Sea View
Camping

**Vicarious
Books**

Special thanks to: Susan Glossop, Gill Sadler, Dave Brodley, Grenville Weston, Russ and Mandy Valentine, Janice Sadler, Pami Hoggatt.

First published in Great Britain by Brian M. Leahy, 2006.

Reprinted 2007. Republished 2008. This edition published September 2010.

© Vicarious Books 2007, 2010.

ISBN: 978-0-9552808-9-4

Vicarious Books, 62 Tontine Street, Folkestone, Kent, CT20 1JP. Tel: 0131 2083333
www.VicariousBooks.co.uk

Editors: Meli George and Chris Doree

Design and artwork by: Chris Gladman Design Tel: 07745 856652

Front cover
Main picture: View from Beeston Regis Caravan and Camping Park.
Small pictures: Sandy Gulls Caravan Park, Sandaway Beach Holiday Park, Damage Barton.

Back cover
Main picture: Folkstone Camping and Caravanning Club Site.
Small Pictures: Bron-Y-Wendon, Ayr Holiday Park.

INTRODUCTION

Welcome to Sea View Camping

Truly breathtaking sea views really make exhilarating starts to your day. As your breakfast sizzles on the stove, you hear the waves crashing on the beach, the rising sun warms the dew on the grass and you sit back and wonder why you ever went to work. If that sounds appealing, then you picked up the right book.

This unique guide shows you all the sea view campsites around Great Britain. All you have to do is choose where you want to go and be ready for a fantastic time as you explore one of the most diverse coastlines in the world. There are campsites perched on the edge of fantastic Jurassic cliff tops, some right on deserted sandy beaches surrounded by hundreds of acres of dunes, and others with every convenience a family could desire. If you love being by the sea, then this is the guide for you.

All the sea view campsites and parks around mainland Great Britain have been included in this guide, so there is sure to be something to suit everyone's needs. Everything from small five pitch sites, to 28 day camping fields, to large holiday parks, and everything in between, is listed in this guide. That way, you are sure to choose the right site for you.

To help you make informed choices, a photo of the sea view from each inspected site is included in the listing. Descriptions are given about the sites, their facilities and amenities, and especially whether beach access is possible. In addition, the location of the nearest pub, shop, beach and slipway is provided to further aid your choice.

Putsborough Sands, Devon

Sand Castles at Sunrise

Welsh Coastal Path

Traeth
Porth Neigwl
(Treheli)
Beach

Gallwch ddilyn Llwybr
Arfordir Llŷn drwy gerdded
ar hyd y traeth hwn.

You can follow the
Llŷn Coastal Path by walking
along this beach.

Gofal	Caution
Byddwch yn wyliadwrus o'r llanw.	Be aware of tidal conditions.
Peidiwch â dringo creigiau na chlogwyni.	Do not climb rocks or cliffs.
Cymerwch ofal arbennig yn ystod tywydd stormus.	Take extra care during stormy weather.

View from Lizard Peninsula, Cornwall

CONTENTS

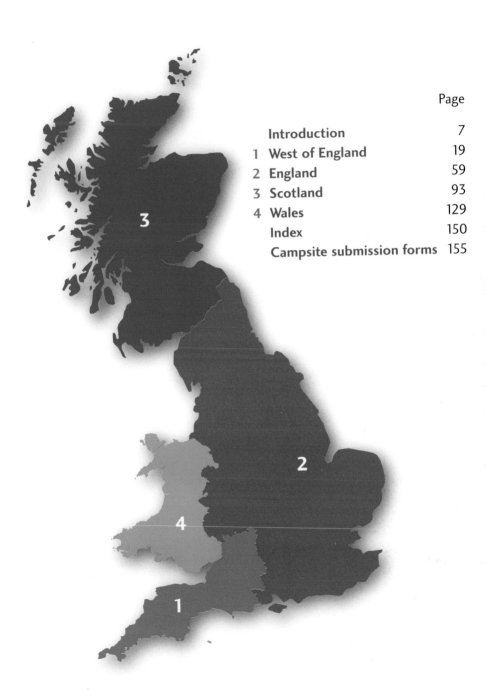

Mussels and Mushrooms

Lifebuoy, Somerset

High Sand Creek Campsite

ABOUT THIS GUIDE

Origins of this guide

Brian M Leahy first published *Sea View Camping* in 2004. Like you, he wanted to be near the sea as he camped around Great Britain. Because he could not find a suitable campsite guide, he decided to travel around the coast and write one himself. For the second edition, Brian selected his favourite 150 sites and produced a full colour, photographed guide. In 2007, Vicarious Books took over the title and developed it into what you are reading today. Brian's favourite 150 sites were re-inspected and a further 100 campsites are listed at the back of the four regions in this book. For this edition, 38 inspected sites have been added to the England section. Undoubtedly, many of the text only listings also have excellent sea views and facilities, but these provide something to discover for the more adventurous camper. Please remember to take photos and fill in the submission forms at the rear of this guide for any sites you feel deserve a more substantial mention.

Campsite selection and inspection

Every campsite with a known sea view has been included in this guide. Campsites are listed on this basis alone, so big or small, if the sea can be seen that's it. Campsites cannot pay to be included or become a featured site in the guide, nor do we just take their word for it. All featured sites are inspected to check the view, as well as the facilities and amenities. The quality or quantity of facilities and amenities are not formally judged, but are simply listed with comments. You can be the judge of what is right for you. In this edition, there are campsites in the England section that do not have any sea views. These were added simply because there are so few sea view sites on that coastline. All the non sea view sites are right by the beach.

Consistency of inspections

Our inspectors are some of the most experienced and knowledgeable campers in the country, regularly travelling throughout the UK and Europe. Their expertise has been used to evaluate the campsites and offer you useful and comprehensive overviews. Inspections were carried out in August, when campsites are at their busiest and under the most pressure. Only three inspectors were commissioned, each covering a specific geographical area.

Inspector profile

Don and Maureen Madge: Never at home for long, Don and Maureen regularly travel the length and breadth of Europe. They toured Scotland for the fourth time to inspect sites for *Sea View Camping*, they also inspected sites in northern England.

Andy and Nette Clarke: When not out and about, Andy is busy running his excellent website www.ukmotorhomes.net. *Sea View Camping* had them touring and inspecting sites in Wales.

Chris Doree and Meli George: The editors of this guide are regular travellers in Europe when not behind their desks at Vicarious Books, Folkestone HQ. They travelled around the West Country and the east coast inspecting sites.

Vicarious Books

Vicarious Books is a publisher and importer of unique motorhome and camping guides. For a list of guides available from Vicarious Books, see the inside front cover of this guide or visit www.VicariousBooks.co.uk.

Scottish Ruins

Land's End, Cornwall

Wheal Coates Tin Mine, St Agnes, Cornwall

Nicholaston Farm Caravan and Camping Site, Penmaen, Swansea

Freshly Caught Seafood Supper

Open Air Theatre, Folkestone, Kent

THE LIZARD POINT GIFT SHOP

Fishing in Kent

HOW TO USE THIS GUIDE

Campsite locator - This guide is split into four colour coded, geographical regions: West of England, England, Scotland, and Wales. Maps are located at the beginning of each region. The numbers printed on the maps identify and locate each campsite. On the opposite page of each regional map is the name and page number of each campsite, given against the corresponding map reference number. Campsites are listed geographically and in map number order, with the text only listings in the same order at the back of each section. The corresponding map reference number is printed beside the campsite name for cross-reference.

Entry explanation

1 **Campsite name**

2 **Campsite map reference number**

3 **Campsite address and phone number**

4 **Campsite website** – where available

5 **Photo from campsite of sea view**

6 **Units accepted by campsite**

   Å   *Tent*

   Touring caravan

   Motorhome

   Large vehicles - Motorhomes/Caravans/5th Wheels. Campsites were checked for accessibility and the owners/managers were asked whether large vehicles were accommodated onsite. Access should be possible for competent and experienced drivers. Most campsites only accept very large vehicles with advanced bookings and we insist that you discuss access and pitch availability with campsite staff before arrival.

   Holiday accommodation for hire – Many of the campsites in this guide have other accommodation for hire (i.e. static caravans, holiday homes, chalets, or lodges). This accommodation has not been inspected and may not have the sea view described in the listing.

7 **Description** – An unbiased description is given of the site and the sea view. The strengths or weaknesses and appeal of the site are provided. Further useful information is also given.

8 **Symbols** – The following symbols are used to identify the size and facilities of the site. All sites have a water tap and a toilet disposal point unless otherwise stated. Facility only available when highlighted.

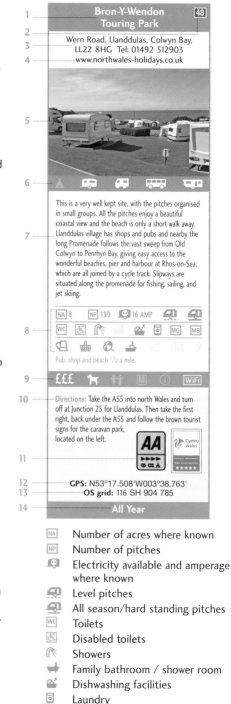

1   **Bron-Y-Wendon Touring Park**   **48**

2

3   Wern Road, Llanddulas, Colwyn Bay, LL22 8HG Tel: 01492 512903

4   www.northwales-holidays.co.uk

5

6   Å

This is a very well kept site, with the pitches organised in small groups. All the pitches enjoy a beautiful coastal view and the beach is only a short walk away. Llanddulas village has shops and pubs and nearby the long Promenade follows the vast sweep from Old Colwyn to Penrhyn Bay, giving easy access to the wonderful beaches, pier and harbour at Rhos-on-Sea, which are all joined by a cycle track. Slipways are situated along the promenade for fishing, sailing, and jet skiing.

7

   NA 8   NP 130   16 AMP

8   WC

Pub, shop and beach ¹/₂ a mile.

9   £££   M   ⓘ   WiFi

10   **Directions:** Take the A55 into north Wales and turn off at Junction 25 for Llanddulas. Then take the first right, back under the A55 and follow the brown tourist signs for the caravan park, located on the left.

   AA   Cymru Wales

11

12   **GPS:** N53°17.508'W003°38.763'
13   **OS grid:** 116 SH 904 785

14   **All Year**

NA	Number of acres where known
NP	Number of pitches
	Electricity available and amperage where known
	Level pitches
	All season/hard standing pitches
WC	Toilets
	Disabled toilets
	Showers
	Family bathroom / shower room
	Dishwashing facilities
	Laundry

10

HOW TO USE THIS GUIDE

[MG] Motorhome grey water disposal

[MB] Motorhome toilet waste disposal

The following symbols identify amenities that are either onsite or within five minutes walk, unless otherwise indicated. The facilities have not been tested and charges may apply.

⊞ Pub/bar

⊞ Shop

Ⓐ Beach

⚓ Slipway

� Indoor or Outdoor swimming pool

/⚑\ Children's play area

⚘ Footpath

9 **Information Symbols**

Cost – The cost of the campsite is indicated by the £ symbols. All prices are based on two people in one caravan or motorhome with electric in August. Prices are offered as a guideline only and should always be confirmed in advance.

£ Up to £10 per night

££ £10-17 per night

£££ £17-35 per night

££££ £35 plus per night

🐕 Many campsites allow dogs onsite, indicated by the dog symbol, but confirmation must always be sought in advance that your dog(s) can be accommodated. Many campsites charge extra for dogs, there may be a limit on the number of dogs allowed onsite, and some sites specify the type of units that dogs can be accommodated in. Some sites also have breed restrictions, so always check your breed is permitted before arrival. Campsite owners and other holidaymakers expect dogs to be kept quiet and under control, and usually on a lead, at all times. Dogs must be exercised in appropriate areas, or offsite, and all mess must be cleared in a responsible fashion. In addition, it is advised that you never leave your dog unattended.

†† This symbol refers to adult only campsites. No person under the age of 18 will be admitted.

[M] This symbol refers to member only campsites. Generally these belong to either the Camping and Caravanning Club or the Caravan Club and a valid membership is required to stay, though it may be possible to join at reception. The name of the club is usually indicated in the title of the campsite. CS and CL sites are also for members only.

CS (Certified Sites) - These sites are for Camping and Caravanning Club members only. These are small sites, restricted to five caravans or motorhomes, plus tents space permitting.

CL (Certified Locations) - These sites are for Caravan Club members only. These are small sites, restricted to five caravans or motorhomes.

ⓘ Internet available (charges may apply).

[WiFi] WiFi available (charges may apply).

10 **Directions** – Directions are provided. Please note that many campsites near the sea are down narrow lanes with passing places.

11 **Awards** – Awards by the tourist board and the AA are indicated here. See page 12 for more information on the award systems.

12 **GPS Co-ordinates** – These are presented in the N53°17.508'W003°38.763' format and were taken at the site entrance. Please note that directions should always be checked when using a satellite navigation machine, as they may not select the best route for your unit. Postcodes do not always provide accurate destinations when used with satellite navigators.

13 **OS grid references** – These refer to the Ordinance Survey Landranger 1:50,000 maps. The first three numbers and the two letters refers to the map identification code, the remaining numbers create a six-figure grid reference.

14 **Opening dates** – Opening dates change year to year and are given as an indication only, please check with the campsite before arrival.

Text only listings – At the end of each chapter there are text only listings for sites that have not been inspected since 2004. The name, address, phone number, web address and directions are included. It is believed that all these sites had a sea view in 2004, however things change and campers are advised to check with the campsite before arrival to avoid disappointment.

HOW TO USE THIS GUIDE

Awards

Visit Britain and the AA inspect holiday, touring and camping parks around Britain.

Visit Britain – The Visit Britain team of professional assessors visit each park every year. They spend time at the park checking all the facilities and award a quality score for every aspect. Parks don't miss out on stars by not having certain facilities, but what they do offer customers must be of the very highest standard in order to receive the top ratings.

All holiday parks with this star rating will meet the minimum standards, which include, among other things: All statutory obligations including site licence, public liability and fire and safety requirements. Minimum quality standards of maintenance and cleanliness as set out by tourism assessing bodies. Provide toilet and washing facilities with hot and cold running water.

Visit Britain rates caravan and camping sites and parks from one to five stars. More stars indicate a greater level of facilities and/or quality.

★ Simple, practical, no frills

★★ Well presented and well run

★★★ Good level of quality and comfort

★★★★ Excellent standard throughout

★★★★★ Exceptional with a degree of luxury

The AA Pennant scheme – The AA's Pennant rating scheme has a five-point scale based on the site's style and the range of facilities. As the Pennant rating increases, so the quality and variety of facilities and amenities is greater. The AA Pennant rating is only based on the touring pitches and the facilities at campsites and caravan parks. AA inspectors do not visit or report on rented static caravans or chalets.

► A simple standard of facilities

►► A better level of facilities, services, customer care and maintenance

►►► A very good standard with well maintained facilities and grounds

►►►► An extremely high standard in all areas

►►►►► An extremely high standard. Facilities, security and customer care are exceptional

Bay View Farm, Cornwall. *Photo campsite owner.*

Cliff House Caravan Park

Land's End, Cornwall

Burnham-on-Sea, Somerset

Norfolk Windmill

Tank Defences

14

Beach Winch

Looe Harbour, Cornwall

Life Boat at Land's End, Cornwall

Heather on Exmoor, Devon

Sunset from North Hill, Somerset

ag Path, Folkestone Coastal Park, Kent

Footpath to Land's End, Cornwall

17

Crail Harbour, near Sauchope Links Caravan Park, Fife © Keith & Natalie Williams

Seaview Holiday Park, Mersea Island, Essex

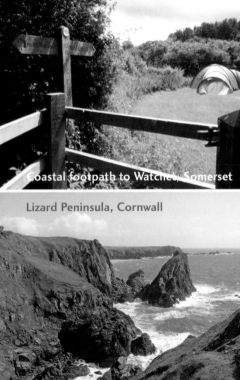

Coastal footpath to Watchet, Somerset

Lizard Peninsula, Cornwall

Woolacombe Bay, Devon

The Lost Gardens of Heligan, Cornwall

ENGLAND THE WEST

Cornish Harbour

The Eden Project, Cornwall

St Michael's Mount, Cornwall

**Wheal Coates Tin Mine, St Agnes, Cornwall
Near Beacon Cottage Farm Campsite**

Bedruthan steps between Newquay and Padstow © *Caroline Stacey*

Blackpool Sands, Devon

WEST OF ENGLAND

Main entries

Text entries at the rear

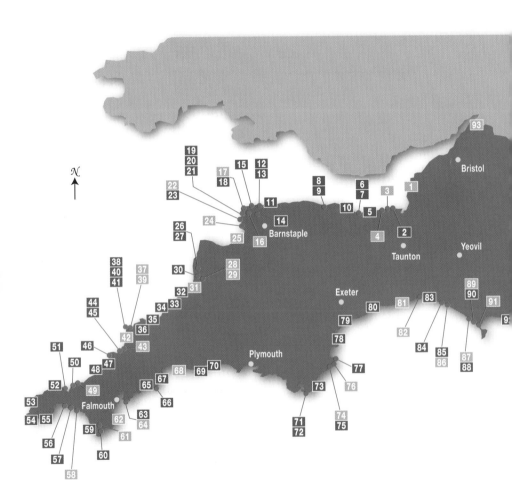

N

93

Bristol

19
20
21

15

12
13

17
18

22
23

8
9

6
7

3

1

11

10

5

26
27

24

14

25

16

Barnstaple

Yeovil

38
40
41

37
39

30

28
29

4

2

Taunton

44
45

32 31

34 33

35

36

42

43

51

46

50

48 47

49

52

53

54 55

Falmouth

62 63
64

59

61

56

60

57

58

31

Exeter

80

81

83

89
90

91

9

79

78

82

84

85
86

87
88

65 67
68 69 70

66

Plymouth

77

73

76

71
72

74
75

WEST OF ENGLAND

2

Staple Farm CL

West Quantoxhead, Taunton, Somerset,
TA4 4EA Tel: 01984 632495
www.caravanclub.co.uk

Situated on the western end of the Quantock Hills, this one acre sloping paddock is part of a traditional working farm. There are good views over the Somerset countryside to the Bristol Channel and Minehead, located at the foot of North Hill. The sand and shingle tidal estuary beaches are a long walk, or a short drive, away.

NA 2   NP 5

Pub and shop 400m.

£££   M   WiFi

Directions: Travelling on the A39 from Bridgwater to Minehead, turn left in West Quantoxhead, immediately past the Windmill Inn. Drive 250 yards uphill going straight over the crossroads and the farm is 50 yards on the right.

GPS: N51°09.950'W003°16.495'
OS grid: 181 ST 109 415

April - October

5

Helwell Bay Holidays

Watchet, Somerset, TA23 0UG
Tel: 01948 631781
www.helwellbay.co.uk

Helwell Bay is a traditional site occupying a narrow cliff top strip right on the Bristol Channel, with views along the Somerset coastline and across to Wales. The 12 touring pitches at the site entrance do not have quite as good sea views as the single line of static caravans that are available for hire. The fossil rich beach is two minutes walk. Trains on the West Somerset Steam Railway chug past immediately behind the site. The quaint harbour town of Watchet is five minutes walk away. From here you can catch the train to Minehead or Bishops Lydeard near Taunton.

NA 6   NP 12   10 AMP

WC

Pub 100m.

£££   M   WiFi

Directions: Drive to Williton on either the A358 from Taunton, or the A39, and take the B3191 at the bottom of Williton High Street. Turn right at the Masons Arms. Follow this road to the end and turn left. As you enter Watchet the sea is on your right. Follow the road until you see the Helwell Bay Holidays sign by the second small turning on the right.

GPS: N51°10.863'W003°19.370'
OS grid: 181 ST 077 432

March - October

6 Warren Bay Holiday Village

Watchet, Somerset, TA23 0JR
Tel: 01984 631460
www.pringsholidayparks.co.uk

The site entrance, with reception on one side and a heated indoor pool on the other, does not seem to prepare you for the amazing journey to the cliff top camping field. 250 mobile homes are set on terraces amongst native and exotic trees and shrubs. Over 200 bird species have been seen on and around the site. The triangular camping field has its long side adjacent to the cliff, and the higher and narrower you go the better the view. There are very good facilities and a steep path to the private stony and mudflat beach.

| NA | 28 | NP | 150 | 16 AMP |

| WC | | | | | | |

Pub and shop at Watchet.

£££

Directions: 1 1/4 miles west of Watchet off the B3191.

GPS: N51°10.657'W003°20.999'
OS grid: 181 ST 058 430

Easter - October

7 Warren Farm

Watchet, Somerset, TA23 0JP
Tel: 01984 631220

This campsite is as old as the hills, well not quite but it was established 1928, and is part of a 260 acre farm. The site spreads over several fields, each area offering a different view and atmosphere but all having plenty of space. The site owners are charming and drive around the extensive site in the mornings, delivering papers and provisions. There are two toilet blocks and, though they are not state of the art, they are well maintained and immaculately kept.

| NA | 14 | NP | 100 | 0 AMP |

| WC | | | | | | |

Pub, shop, beach and slipway at Watchet.

£££

Directions: 1 1/2 miles west of Watchet off the B3191.

GPS: N51°10.718'W003°21.547'
OS grid: 181 ST 050 431

Easter - October

8
Home Farm Campsite

Blue Anchor, Minehead, Somerset, TA24 6JS
Tel: 01984 640817
www.homefarmblueanchor.co.uk

Home Farm is a small working livestock farm adjacent to the sea, but is behind a sea wall and a road, so has no sea views. There is a huge tide in the Bristol Channel and the sand and pebble beach can be vast or nonexistent. This means the water is warm and shallow and there is good rock pooling. The campsite owners organise one of the best summer boot fairs in the country: Saturdays 2 - 5pm. Blue Anchor has two real ale pubs and the one onsite offers good food. The campsite has a pleasant tearoom and there is a seafront café. This is a member's only site, affiliated to the Camping and Caravanning Club, but you can join on arrival.

NA 2   NP 20   10 AMP

WC

Pub onsite. Shop onsite. Slipway 150m.

£££   M   i   WiFi

Directions: Travelling west on the A39 from Bridgwater, drive through Washford and after half a mile take the first right onto the B3191, signposted 'Blue Anchor', 'Old Cleeve' and 'Chapel Cleeve'. Drive to the end of the road, to the Blue Anchor pub, and turn left along the seafront. The farm entrance is 300m on the left and shares its entrance with the Smugglers Inn.

GPS: N51°10.953'W003°23.406'
OS grid: 181 ST 029 435

April - October

9
Hoburn Blue Anchor

Blue Anchor Bay, Nr. Minehead, Somerset, TA24 6JT Tel: 01643 821360
www.hoburne.com/blueanchor_main.asp

This family friendly holiday park is set in open fields adjacent to the sea, but most of the site is lower than the sea wall and there is no sea view from the touring field. Blue Anchor Bay offers an expansive sea view all the way to the tip of Wales on a clear day. The park has an indoor leisure pool, crazy golf, and outdoor adventure playground. The onsite convenience store also sells tackle and bait. Fishing from the sea wall is popular, and dogfish are often caught. The cliff walk to Watchet is lovely and you can catch a steam train back to Blue Anchor.

NA 13   NP 113   10 AMP

WC

Pub 100m. Shop onsite. Slipway 300m.

£££   M   i   WiFi

Directions: Travelling west on the A39 from Bridgwater, drive through Washford and after half a mile take the first right onto the B3191, signposted 'Blue Anchor', 'Old Cleeve' and 'Chapel Cleeve'. Drive to the end of the road, to the Blue Anchor pub, and turn left along the seafront. The farm entrance is 500m on the left and is clearly signed.

GPS: N51°10.940'W003°23.823'
OS grid: 181 ST 024 434

April - October

Minehead Camping and Caravanning Club Site 〔10〕

Hill Road, North Hill, Minehead, Somerset,
TA24 5LB Tel: 01643 704138
www.siteseeker.co.uk

This site is perched high above Minehead on North Hill, part of Exmoor National Park. Not every pitch has sea views, but the location is stunning. Unfortunately, trees are reducing the sea view every year and it is a long walk to the beach or to Minehead. However, walkers need only walk out of the gate to set foot on the moor and see the ponies.

| NA 3 | NP 60 | ☻ 16 AMP | | |

| WC | ♿ | ♺ | 🛁 | 🍴 | ○ | MG | MB |

Pub, shop, beach and slipway at Minehead.

£££ 🐕 👫 M ⓘ WiFi

Directions: From the A39 either direction, drive to Minehead town centre not to the seafront. At Wellington Square opposite HSBC bank, turn into the High Street (The Parade) and take the second left into Blenheim Road and the next left into Martlet Road. Keep left at the church following a narrow, steep and twisty road for one mile to the site, which is on the right. No Caravans allowed.

GPS: N51°12.834'W003°29.680'
OS grid: 181 SS 958 471

May - September

Napps Camping and Touring Holidays 〔11〕

Old Coast Road, Berrynarbor, North Devon,
EX34 9SW Tel: 01271 882557
www.napps.co.uk

Delightfully located in an area of outstanding natural beauty, this is a really pleasant and quiet touring and tenting only site. The pitching areas are terraced into the hillside, providing increasingly beautiful views the higher you climb. There is an outdoor heated pool, a nice bar and grill, a well stocked shop and superb toilets. The sea is only 10 minutes away, down 220 steps.

| NA 45 | NP 200 | ☻ 10 AMP | | |

| WC | ♿ | ♺ | 🛁 | 🍴 | ○ | MG | MB |

Pub, shop, beach and slipway 400m at Watermouth.

£££ 🐕 👫 M ⓘ WiFi

Directions: Two miles southwest of Combe Martin and three miles east of Ilfracombe on the A399. The site owner advises that you avoid Barnstaple as it is often congested, and that you avoid the A39 coastal route from Minehead and Porlock as the road is narrow and extremely steep in parts.

GPS: N51°12.512'W004°03.863'
OS grid: 180 SS 559 479

March - October

12 Damage Barton

Mortehoe, Woolacombe, North Devon,
EX34 7EJ Tel: 01271 870502
www.damagebarton.co.uk

© Helen Lethbridge

A park of two halves, this site is affiliated to both the caravan clubs and maintains a high standard across the entire park. Just about every pitch has great sea views as far as the Welsh coast. Tractor tours of the 580 acre National Trust land and family run farm operate from May to September. Lee Bay is 1¹/₂ miles away, about a 25 minute walk, and there is a bus stop conveniently located at the campsite entrance.

| NA | 16 | NP | 150 | 10 AMP |

| WC | | | | | MG |

Pub and shop at Morthoe. Beach at Woolacombe.

£££

Directions: From Barnstaple, travel 10 miles toward Ilfracombe on the A316. At the Mullacott Cross roundabout turn left onto the B3343 towards Woolacombe. In 1³/₄ miles turn right, signed 'Mortehoe' and campsite name, into Mortehoe Station Road. Travel one mile and the campsite entrance is on the right, clearly signed.

GPS: N51°11.025'W004°11.312'
OS grid: 180 SS 471 451

March - October

13 Sandaway Beach Holiday Park

Woodlands, Coombe Martin, North Devon,
EX24 0AS Tel: 01271 866766
www.johnfowlerholidays.com

From many of the holiday homes on this park there are excellent sea views, though no view is available from the small touring area. A small tent area set amongst trees does have a nice view through a break in the trees. The best views are enjoyed from the bar and as you explore the park. Three minutes walk down a picturesque, stepped path brings you to Sandaway Beach, which is privately owned by the campsite.

| NA | 20 | NP | 20 | 10 AMP |

| WC | | | |

Pub, shop and slipway 1¹/₂ miles at Watermouth Cove.

£££

Directions: The campsite is located adjacent to the A399 a quarter of a mile northwest of Combe Martin.

GPS: N51°12.377'W004°02.690'
OS grid: 180 SS 571 471

March - November

14
Sunnymead Farm

Mullacott, Ilfracombe, Devon EX34 8NZ
Tel: 01271 879845
http://sunnymead-farm.co.uk

This site offers some of the least expensive camping in the area, which is fair as it is not as well located as other local sites. There are two level paddocks alongside the busy B3343, these cater for five tourers, and plenty of tents. 10 electric hook-ups are available. A new shower and toilet block was commissioned in 2010. There is a distant view of the sea across farmland.

| NA | 1¹/₂ | NP | 30 | 💀 16 AMP |

| WC |

Pub 1 mile. New shower/toilet block 2010.

£££ 🐕 ‡‡ M ⓘ WiFi

Directions: From Barnstaple, travel 10 miles toward Ilfracombe on the A316. At the Mullacott Cross roundabout turn left onto the B3343 towards Woolacombe. The site is approximately half a mile on the right-hand side, just past the Veterinary Hospital, opposite the Highways Guest House.

GPS: N51°10.640'W004°08.793'
OS grid: 180 SS 499 442

Easter - October

15
Easewell Farm Holiday Park

Mortehoe, Woolacombe, Devon, EX34 7EH
Tel: 01271 870343
www.woolacombe.co.uk

max 28ft

Having driven around the beautifully kept nine hole golf course you arrive at the top of the campsite and can immediately appreciate the sea views that you will enjoy during your holiday. Laid out in terraces, the top most camping areas at the entrance command the best views. This is a luxury site with excellent facilities including a heated indoor pool, indoor bowls, snooker, golf, children's play area, restaurant and licensed club.

| NA | 30 | NP | 300 | 💀 16 AMP |

| WC |

Beach 15 - 20 minutes.

£££ 🐕 ‡‡ M ⓘ WiFi

Directions: From Barnstaple, travel 10 miles toward Ilfracombe on the A316. At the Mullacott Cross roundabout turn left onto the B3343 towards Woolacombe. In 1.7 miles turn right, signed 'Mortehoe' and campsite name into Mortehoe Station Rd. Travel 1¹/₂ miles and the campsite and golf course entrance is on the right, clearly signed.

GPS: N51°11.237 W004°12.012'
OS grid: 180 SS 462 455

Mid March - October

North Morte Farm Camping and Caravan Park [18]

Mortehoe, Woolacombe, North Devon,
EX34 7EG Tel: 01271 870381
www.northmortefarm.co.uk

Camping here is as it should be, wild but civilised. The site entrance is just off Mortehoe village centre, convenient to shops and restaurants. The camping fields are in the moors, but are all well manicured to enable comfortable camping. The sea views are absolutely stunning and the stargazing is exceptional. There are modern toilet blocks, serviced touring pitches, and static caravans for hire.

NA 25   NP 175   16 AMP

WC

Pub at Mortehoe. Beach 10 minute walk.

£££

Directions: From Barnstaple, travel 10 miles toward Ilfracombe on the A316. At the Mullacott Cross roundabout turn left onto the B3343 towards Woolacombe. In 1.7 miles turn right, signed 'Mortehoe' and campsite name, into Mortehoe Station Rd. Travel 1.9 miles to Mortehoe and turn right into North Morte Road by The Smugglers Rest. The site is 500 yards on the left.

GPS: N51°11.301'W004°12.216'
OS grid: 180 SS 461 457

Easter - October

Europa Park [19]

Beach Road, Woolacombe, Devon,
EX34 7AN Tel: 01271 871425
www.europapark.co.uk

Europa Park is a lively, vibrant site with a great atmosphere and some funky and unique accommodation for hire. This is probably the only campsite in the county that actively encourages Stag and Hen parties. Woolacombe village and beach are a staggering distance. Onsite there are several toilet blocks, a café and late night bar, an indoor pool, sauna, and even a Surfboard Hire caravan. To top it all, there is an awesome sea view towards Lundy that can be seen from most of this terraced site.

NA 16   NP 300   10 AMP

WC

Pub 300m.

£££

Directions: From Barnstaple, travel 10 miles towards Ilfracombe on the A316. At the Mullacott Cross roundabout turn left onto the B3343 towards Woolacombe. Travel 2.7 miles to the site entrance on the right hand side of the road beside a fuel station and Spar, approximately one mile from Woolacombe.

GPS: N51°10.320'W004°11.030'
OS grid: 180 SS 473 437

All Year

Warcombe Farm Camping Park [20]

Station Road, Mortehoe, North Devon,
EX34 7EJ Tel: 01271 870690
www.warcombefarm.co.uk

The site gently slopes towards the sea and is split in two by the carp fishing lake. The top half has the best sea views, stretching across the Bristol Channel. However, some trees have been planted that may obscure the view eventually. The lower part of the park is separated into small hedged areas and the sea can be glimpsed over the Devon hedge from the pitches closest to the sea. The toilet blocks offer exceptional quality normally only found in high-class hotels.

| NA | 19 | | NP | 260 | | 16 AMP | | |

| WC | | | | | | | | MG | | |

Pub, shop, beach and slipway at Woolacombe Bay.

£££

Directions: From Barnstaple, travel 10 miles toward Ilfracombe on the A316. At the Mullacott Cross roundabout turn left onto the B3343 towards Woolacombe. In 1.7 miles turn right, signed 'Mortehoe' and campsite name into Mortehoe Station Rd. Travel 0.6 miles and the campsite is on the right, clearly signed.

GPS: N51°10.771'W004°10.881'
OS grid: 180 SS 478 422

March - October

Woolacombe Bay Holiday Village [21]

Seymour, Sandy Lane, Woolacombe, Devon,
EX34 7AH Tel: 01271 870343
www.woolacombe.com

© Matt Lenster

This is a large, terraced, family park with sea views and a wide range of facilities on offer including: indoor pool, Dunes water park, golf, tennis, bowls as well as relaxation at Club Romano Spa and a lively nightlife. There is a bus to the beach and the sister sites. A footpath also leads to the beach. There are lots of holiday homes for hire, but this site only takes tents on the camping fields (pictured).

| NA | 15 | | NP | 170 | | 16 AMP | | |

| WC | | | | | | | | MG | | |

Pub, shop and beach at Weymouth.

£££

Directions: From Barnstaple, travel 10 miles toward Ilfracombe on the A316. At the Mullacott Cross roundabout turn left onto the B3343 towards Woolacombe. In 1.7 miles turn right, signed 'Mortehoe' and campsite name into Mortehoe Station Rd. Travel 0.7 miles and turn left into Sandy lane, clearly signed, and drive 200m to campsite.

GPS: N51°10.625'W004°11.468'
OS grid: 180 SS 469 435

All Year

WEST OF ENGLAND

23 Putsborough Sands

Putsborough, Georgeham, Nr Braunton,
North Devon, EX33 1LB Tel: 01271 890230
www.putsborough.com

This two acre site is right alongside an enormous sandy surfing beach. The touring caravan only pitches are in an area that is sheltered, with some gently sloping and terraced parts. Small campervans may be able to park near the beach for a fee, but there is no camping for tents on this site. This is an absolutely perfect site for a beach holiday, especially if you like to surf, sail or windsurf. Surfing equipment is available for hire.

| NA 2 | NP 25 | 16 AMP | | |
| WC | | | | |

£££

Directions: The site owners recommend a one-way system, so travel from Braunton on the B3231 through Croyde and continue onto Georgeham. Turn left following signs to Putsborough and Sands. All the roads to the site are narrow so avoid travelling to the site between 4 - 6pm when people are leaving the beach and at 9am and 3pm during school terms.

GPS: N51°08.614'W004°13.198'
OS grid: 180 SS 448 405

April - Mid October

26 Ivyleaf CL

Ivyleaf Farm, Stratton, Bude, Cornwall,
EX23 9LD Tel: 01288 321592
www.ivyleafgolf.com

This CL is way above par. There are five, hard standing, serviced bays, in a hedged corner overlooking the golf course. The views stretch across countryside to the sea in the distance. Being part of, and adjacent to, a golf and mountain boarding centre, campers have use of the toilets, showers and washing machines. Visitors must book in at reception on arrival. Advanced booking is recommended.

| NA 1 | NP 5 | 16 AMP | | |
| WC | | | | |

££

Directions: Located halfway between Kilkhampton and Stratton. From Stratton travel one mile north and turn right, signed 'Ivy Leaf Golf Course'. Drive half a mile up this road and the site is on the left, signed.

GPS: N50°51.129'W004°30.260'
OS grid: 190 SS 241 085

All Year

Penhalt Farm Holiday Park `27`

Widemouth Bay, Poundstock, Bude,
Cornwall EX23 0DG Tel: 01288 361210
www.penhaltfarm.co.uk

Penhalt sits high on the coastal downs, one mile south and 10 minutes walk from Widemouth Bay. Every pitch offers commanding views of the magnificent Atlantic coastline and the beautiful surrounding countryside. This site would be the editor's choice if visiting Widemouth Bay, having a preference for open spaces and simple sites. Two caravans are available to rent. Widemouth Bay is a popular sandy beach good for surfing and swimming.

| NA | 4¹/2 | NP | | 10 AMP | | |

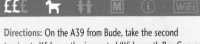

Beach 10 minutes downhill.

££

Directions: On the A39 from Bude, take the second turning to Widemouth, signposted 'Widemouth Bay Caravan Park'. Follow this road until just past the Widemouth Manor pub. Turn left, signed 'Widemouth Bay' and 'Penhalt Farm', follow road for one mile and Penhalt Farm is on the left, clearly signed.

GPS: N50°46.393'W004°33.765'
OS grid: 190 SS 194 003

March - October

Sandymouth Bay Holiday Park `30`

Bude, Cornwall, EX23 9HW
Tel: 01288 352563
www.sandymouthbay.co.uk

This site affords one of the best sea views in the west. From the touring pitches and 10 acre camping field there are awesome panoramic views of both coast and countryside. This is a big family park with lots of quality accommodation and excellent facilities. However, due to the location of the camping area, you feel like you are there on your own. The beach is a 10 minute walk away.

| NA | 25 | NP | 50 | 10 AMP | | |

Pub, shop and slipway at Bude.

££

Directions: Turn off the A39 south of Kirkhampton, signposted 'Sandymouth'. Follow the road for one mile and, after the village of Stibb, turn left, signposted 'Sandymouth Holiday Park' and 'Sandymouth Bay National Trust'. The site is 450m on the left.

GPS: N50°52.012'W004°32.249'
OS grid: 190 SS 217 107

March - September

WEST OF ENGLAND

Widemouth Bay Caravan Park [32]

Poundstock, Bude,Cornwall EX23 0DF
Tel: 01271 866766
www.johnfowlerholidays.com/widemouth.htm

This park is big and lively with 50 acres to explore and an abundance of facilities and amenities. The very popular, mostly sloping camping area is well away from the main park at the top of the hill. From many of the pitches the sea can be seen, but the countryside views are better. Widemouth Bay is a 10 - 15 minute downhill walk away. The sandy bay is very popular because of the good bathing and wonderful surfing.

NA 50	NP 120	16 AMP		
WC				

£££

Directions: Travel three miles south from Bude on the A39 and take the second turning to Widemouth Bay. Travel 0.9 of a mile and turn left beside the Widemouth Manor Hotel, signed. The site entrance is 300m on the left. Turn left into the site road and drive up to reception.

AA
►►►

GPS: N50°46.594'W004°33.153'
OS grid: 190 SS 198 008

March - October

Trewethett Farm Caravan Club Site [33]

Trethevy, Tintagel, PL34 0BQ
Tel: 01840 770222
www.caravanclub.co.uk

This five star site has a five star sea view. Perched directly on the Cornish cliffs, this immaculately kept site offers fantastic luxury and the sea views are as good as they get. The serviced, level touring pitches benefit from being arranged on several terraces, there is even a separate camping field. The sea view is breathtaking from all areas on the site.

| NA 15 | NP 153 | 16 AMP | | |
| WC | | | | | MG | MB |

Pub and slipway at Boscastle. Shop at Tintagel.

£££

Directions: Located directly off the B3263 on exiting Tintagel towards Boscastle, signed on the left.

GPS: N50°40.439'W004°43.606'
OS grid: 200 SX 074 897

March - November

34
The Headland Caravan Park

Atlantic Road, Tintagel, Cornwall, PL34 0DE
Tel: 01840 770239
www.headlandcaravanpark.co.uk

Location, Location, Location! Tintagel, just outside the gate, boasts many pubs, restaurants, tearooms, local shops and attractions. This is a great rest stop for walkers following the coast path, or users of large motorhomes or campers without additional means of transport. There are partial sea views from some areas on this reasonably large, mostly level site.

| NA | 5 | NP | 20 | 16 AMP |

Slipway at Boscastle.

£££

Directions: Drive straight through Tintagel, following signposts to 'headland' and 'caravan park' and the site is on the right before the headland.

GPS: N50°39.995'W004°45.084'
OS grid: 200 SX 055 887

Easter - October

35
Lower Pennycrocker Farm

St. Juliot, Boscastle, Cornwall PL35 0BY
Tel: 01840 250257
www.pennycrocker.com

Spacious and level, this cliff top site is part of a working farm in an absolutely beautiful setting. There are good sea views and wonderful views over 15 miles to Padstow and beyond. Access to the sea is about a 10 minute drive away and from the coast path you can walk to Cornwall's highest cliffs. There are also onsite fishing lakes, which are stocked with carp and tench.

| NA | 6 | NP | 40 | 16 AMP |

££

Directions: Turn off the A39, signposted 'Boscastle', onto the B3263. Travel 2³/₄ miles and turn right off the B3263, signposted 'Lower Pennycrocker Camping'. Follow the signs for half a mile down the narrow, single track road (there are some passing areas). The site is on the left, signed.

AA

GPS: N50°42.212'W004°39.377'
OS grid: 190 SX 125 927

Easter - October

Chapel Farm CL 36

Edmonton, Wadebridge, Cornwall, PL27 7JA
Tel: 01208 812011
www.caravanclub.co.uk

Tucked away in a rural location, this informal, five pitch site is level at the top before sloping away. There are fine countryside views leading on over the estuary, out to sea and across to Padstow. Visitors are trusted to pay in an honesty box. The local country pub is very attractive with an excellent reputation for food, and is only two minutes walk away.

| NA | 1 | NP | 5 | | 0 AMP | | |

Pub 100m. Shop adjacent to A39.

£££

Directions: Travelling towards Truro on the A39, pass Wadebridge and go straight over the Shell/Tesco roundabout. In 200m turn right, signposted 'Edmonton'. Follow the lane for half a mile and pass the Quarryman pub on the right. When the road divides enter the site through the gate that divides both lanes.

GPS: N50°31.131'W004°52.468'
OS grid: 200 SW 963 728

April - October

Mother Ivey's Bay 38

Trevose Head, Nr Padstow,
Cornwall, PL28 8SL Tel: 01841 520990
www.motheriveysbay.com

This is a big holiday park, with lots of holiday homes set closest to the sea. This is a great place for a beach holiday but is also adjacent to Trevose Golf and Country Club. The beach (pictured) is just perfect, tucked away in a small cliff backed cove with soft golden sand. There is a camping field available in the summer that gives good sea views and there are some excellent serviced pitches. The facilities are superb and a great deal of effort has gone into landscaping this park.

| NA | 25 | NP | 175 | | 10 AMP | | |

Pub at Harlyn. Shop and slipway at Padstow.

£££

Directions: From Padstow head southwest towards Newquay on the B3276. In two miles turn right in St Merryn centre, turning left at the crossroads, then take the next right turn in 400 yards, signposted 'Trevose Golf Club'. At the golf club, turn right at the sharp left-hand bend. Turn left at the next junction and Mother Ivey's is second on the right.

GPS: N50°32.473'W005°00.841'
OS grid: 200 SW 865 755

March - October

40 Trethias Farm Caravan Park

Treyarnon Bay, St Merryn, Padstow,
Cornwall PL28 8PL
Tel: 01841 520323

This site is meticulously managed which creates a unique atmosphere. Pitches are placed around the edge of the two large fields, leaving plenty of space for well behaved children to play. Most pitches have a sea view and it is only a few hundred metres to the beach, but there is no vehicle access. The coast path also runs close by.

NA	15	NP	63	10 AMP	

Pub 1 mile. Shop, beach and slipway at Padstow.

£££

Directions: From Padstow head southwest towards Newquay on the B3276, travel through St Merryn and turn second right in 0.8 of a mile, signposted 'Trethias' and camping sign direction 'Treyarnon '. Follow the campsite signs for three quarters of a mile and stop at reception by the farm in the village, which is a significant distance from the campsite. Maximum 8.5m (28 ft) - if you're brave enough.

enjoyEngland.com
★★★
TOURING PARK

GPS: N50°31.365'W005°01.425'
OS grid: 200 SW 856 733

April - September

41 Treyarnon Bay

Padstow, Cornwall, PL28 8JR
Tel; 01841 520681
www.treyarnonbay.co.uk

Adjacent to a small, but popular, sandy beach (pictured), this is a traditional camping and static caravan site. There are several areas with sea views as you move through the park. The camping field has clean, mobile toilet blocks nearby, but is set furthest from the beach and shower block. Site visitors are charged to use the showers, which are also available to beach visitors. The beach is a great place for kids and has a lifeguard in attendance.

NA	10	NP	55	10 AMP	

£££

Directions: From Padstow head southwest towards Newquay on the B3276, travel through St Merryn and turn second right in 0.8 of a mile, signposted 'Trethias' and camping sign and direction 'Treyarnon'. Follow signpost to 'Treyarnon Bay' for one mile. The site entrance is in the beach car park. Large motorhomes are accepted, but access is difficult down the Cornish lanes.

enjoyEngland.com
★★★★
SELF CATERING

GPS: N50°31.660'W005°01.224'
OS grid: 200 SW 858 741

April - September

Tregurrian Camping and Caravanning Club Site |44|

Tregurrian, Near Newquay, Cornwall,
TR8 4AE Tel: 01637 860448
www.siteseeker.co.uk

Library picture

The camping area is in spacious field bordered with hedges and some pitches offer distant views of the sea. Facilities are up to the normal Camping and Caravanning Club standards. Watergate Bay is three quarters of a mile away. There are coastal walks from the site to the glorious sandy beach, which is a haven for water sport lovers.

NA		NP	90		16 AMP		
WC	🦽	🚿	🛁	🛁	⊡	MG	MB
							🚶

Pub 1 mile at Trevarrian.

£££ 🐕 ♦♦ |M| ⓘ |WiFi|

Directions: From the A39 at St Columb Major, take the A3059 towards Newquay, signposted 'Airport'. In one mile, turn right to Watermouth Bay and Airport. Travel 2.8 miles to a T-junction and turn left onto the B3276 towards Newquay. In half a mile turn right, signed 'Tregurrian Campsite' and the site is 200m on the left.

GPS: N50°26.928'W005°02.046'
OS grid: 200 SW 847 654

April - September

Trevean Caravan and Camping Park |45|

Trevean Lane, St Merrryn, Padstow, Cornwall,
PL28 8PR Tel: 01841 520772
www.treveancaravanandcamping.net

This is a very pleasant, small family run campsite on a working farm. From a few pitches there is a distant view of the sea over countryside. The layout and small number of pitches gives a cosy, friendly feel to the campsite. The village of St Merryn is about one mile away, as are the golden sands of Porthcothan, Treyarnon and Constantine bays.

NA	1¹/₂	NP	71		16 AMP		
WC	🦽	🚿	🛁	🛁	⊡		
	🧺					/📐\	

Pub and shop at St Merryn/Porthcothan.

££ 🐕 ♦♦ |M| ⓘ |WiFi|

Directions: From Padstow head southwest towards Newquay on the B3276, travel through St Merryn and turn left in one mile, signposted 'Trevean mile'. The site is 600m on the right, signposted. Maximum 7.5m (25 ft).

GPS: N50°30.742'W004°59.801'
OS grid: 200 SW 874 724

April - October

Beacon Cottage Farm Touring Park 46

Beacon Drive, St Agnes, Cornwall, TR5 0NU
Tel: 01872 552347 / 07879 413862
www.beaconcottagefarmholidays.co.uk

© Jane Sawle

As you enter the site, you pass by beautifully kept stone farm buildings, now used by the campsite, that make up part of this traditional, working Cornish family farm. There are some very secluded and cosy pitching spots, but the two main camping fields give excellent cliff and sea views as far as St Ives. This is a family friendly site located on the South West Coast Path, with the captivating remains of Wheal Coates tin mine just 200m away. Walkers welcome.

NA 4	NP 60	10 AMP		
WC				

Pub and shop 2 miles at St Agnes.

£££

Directions: From the A30, turn right at the Chiverton roundabout onto B3277, signposted 'St Agnes'. In three miles, past Presingoll Barns turn left at the mini roundabout, signposted 'Chapel Porth'. In four miles turn left where you see a brown tourism sign to Beacon Cottage Farm. Follow these signs to the park, approximately one mile. Narrow with some passing areas.

GPS: N50°18.339'W005°13.515'
OS grid: 203 SW 703 501

April - September

Trevellas Manor Farm 47

Cross Combe, St Agnes, Cornwall, TR5 0XP
Tel: 01872 552238

Simply perfect and perfectly simple, this camping field gently slopes towards the wonderful sea view and the surrounding rolling countryside is dotted with bygone tin mines. St Agnes, about 1½ miles away, has local shops and restaurants and the beach is a one mile downhill walk away. The simple facilities, located by the farmhouse, are opposite the entrance to camping field.

NA 6	NP 35	10 AMP		
WC				

Pub and shop at St Agnes/Mithian.

£££

Directions: From St Agnes travel one mile towards Perranporth on the B3285 and turn left, signposted 'Cross Combe'. Do not take the 'Airport' or 'School' turning. Follow the road for 1.2 miles down a narrow lane, with some passing areas, and the campsite is on the left.

GPS: N50°19.276'W005°11.188'
OS grid: 203 SW 731 517

April - October

St Agnes Beacon Caravan Club Site [48]

Beacon Drive, St Agnes, Cornwall, TR5 0NU
Tel: 01872 552543
www.caravanclub.co.uk

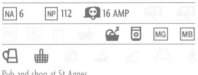

Old quarries seem to naturally convert into great campsites, and this site certainly benefits from its long lost industrial past. Situated at the foot of the Beacon, there are good views of the Cornish coastline. Much of the site is gently sloping and arranged on several levels, partly sheltered by gorse-topped banking. There is no toilet block, but high standards are maintained across the site, which has the usual club feel. Maximum 9.2 metres (30 ft).

| NA | 6 | NP | 112 | 16 AMP | | |

| WC | | | 🗄 | MG | MB |

🔌 🧺

Pub and shop at St Agnes.

£££ 🐕 †† M ⓘ WiFi

Directions: Right next to Beacon Cottage Farm. From the A30 at Chiverton roundabout, take the B3277 to St Agnes. Turn left as you enter St Agnes. In 1¼ miles, over the crossroads, fork right into Beacon Drive. The site is the second tarmac driveway on the right.

GPS: N50°18.448'W005°13.534'
OS grid: 203 SW 705 502

April - September

Beachside Holiday Park [50]

Hayle, Cornwall, TR27 5AW
Tel: 01736 753080
www.beachside.co.uk

Nestled amongst hundreds of acres of sand dunes, this unique campsite occupies 20 acres. Some pitching areas are gently sloping and all are spread through an amazing complex of sand dunes that any child would love to play within. Not all the pitches have views, but from some you can see the sea stretching to St Ives. There is plenty to explore and there is direct access to an enormous, quiet sandy beach via a walkway leading through the dunes. Closest to the sea, there is a small complex of retro holiday chalets for hire.

| NA | 20 | NP | 80 | 10 AMP | | |

| WC | ♿ | 🚿 | | 🗄 | | |

🔌 🚰 🅿 🏊 🎢 🚶

£££ 🐕 †† M ⓘ WiFi

Directions: Exit the A30 at the large roundabout north of Hayle (McDonalds and Next) and take the road into Hayle, signposted 'Hayle B3301/Helston B3302'. After half a mile turn right by the putting green, signposted 'Phillack and Towans Beaches'. Follow the brown tourist signs to the site.

GPS: N50°12.132'W005°24.903'
OS grid: 203 SW 564 389

Easter - September

51
Ayr Holiday Park
St Ives, Cornwall, TR26 1EJ
Tel: 01736 795855
www.ayrholidaypark.co.uk

This campsite is conveniently located in the suburbs high above St Ives. The elevated position enables excellent views across St Ives bay, from most touring pitches and static caravans. During the day you can watch the surfers and swimmers, at night the illuminations set the scene. St Ives harbour is a half a mile downhill walk away; thankfully you can catch a bus back. The campsite facilities are exceptionally good and there are local shops and pubs close by. Unsurprisingly, this is a popular site.

| NA 10 | NP 68 | 16 AMP | | |

| WC | | | | | MG | |

Pub, shop, beach and slipway at St Ives.

£££

Directions: Pass Hayle on the A30 then take the St Ives exit. In 350m turn left at the second mini roundabout following signs to St Ives for heavy vehicles. After three miles turn right at the T-junction onto the B3311. Travel one mile through Halsetown and turn right at the B3306 T-junction to St Ives. In 700m turn left onto Carnellis Road at the first of two mini roundabouts, signposted 'Ayr and Porthmeor beach'. Follow the road for 800m through a housing estate to the park entrance on left, after a sharp 'S' bend.

GPS: N50°12.752'W005°29.372'
OS grid: 203 SW 511 405

All Year

52
Trevalgan Touring Park
St Ives, Cornwall, TR26 3BJ
Tel: 01736 792048
www.trevalgantouringpark.co.uk

This is the sister site to the excellently located Ayr Holiday Park in St Ives, both are beautifully maintained with excellent facilities. Where Ayr is great for younger campers this site is great for families and people wishing to relax and unwind, there is even a designated area for backpackers. There are views across countryside to the sea from many pitches. A bus stops onsite from June - mid September taking campers the two miles to St Ives.

| NA 5 | NP 132 | 16 AMP | | |

| WC | | | | | MG | |

Pub and beach at St Ives. Shop on site.

£££

Directions: Pass Hayle on the A30 then take the St Ives exit. In 350m turn left at the second mini roundabout following signs to St Ives for heavy vehicles. After three miles turn right at the T-junction onto the B3311. Travel one mile through Halsetown and turn left at the B3306 T-junction. Travel half a mile and turn right (brown tourist sign) to the campsite. Take the right fork in half a mile, then drive 300m to the site.

GPS: N50°12.468'W005°31.136'
OS grid: 203 SW 490 401

All Year

WEST OF ENGLAND

Trevedra Farm Caravan and Camping Site 53

Sennen, Penzance, Cornwall, TR19 7BE
Tel: 01736 871835/18
www.cornwall-online.co.uk/trevedra/Welcome.html

Trevedra campsite has been family run for over 70 years and is part of a working farm. There are three camping areas, one for Caravan Club members, one for the general public and a walkers and tent camping field. The facilities are modern and well cared for. Sennen Cove and Gwenver sandy surf beaches are about 15 minutes walk away and both have lifeguards in attendance. Land's End is within walking distance along the coast path.

NA 12	NP 200	🔌 16 AMP		
WC	♿	📷	🍽 ⬚	MG
🚿	🛒	🔍		🚶

Pub, shop and beach at Sennen.

£££ 🐕 🚻 M ⓘ WiFi

Directions: Take the A30 from Penzance to Land's End, pass through the village of Crows-an-Wra, passing the Chapel on your right. Just after the turn off to St Just, B3306 (also on your right), take the first right at the sign to Trevedra Farm.

GPS: N50°05.282'W005°40.735'
OS grid: 203 SW 369 274

April - October

Sennen Cove Camping and Caravanning Club Site 54

Higher Tregiffian Farm, St Buryan, Penzance, Cornwall, TR19 6JB Tel: 01736 871588
www.siteseeker.co.uk

This is a small, gently sloping, well maintained site. The sea can be seen over the hedges and attractive farmland. Walking to the beach takes you down a steep one mile path with steps. You can also walk to Land's End on the coast path, where there are pubs, restaurants and amusements. Aircraft noise can be heard on site, but can be appreciated if you take a scenic flight in a Cessna. See www.islesofscilly-travel.co.uk for information.

NA 3	NP 72	🔌 16 AMP		
WC	♿	📷	🍽 ⬚	MG	MB
🚿	🛒			🚶

Pub and shop at St Just.

£££ 🐕 🚻 M ⓘ WiFi

Directions: From St Just head towards Land's End on the B3306. The site is on the right just past Land's End Airport, signed.

GPS: N50°05.381'W005°40.150'
OS grid: 203 SW 375 276

May - September

55
Kemyel Crease CL

Paul, Penzance, Cornwall. TR19 6NP
Tel: 01736 731589
www.caravanclub.co.uk

This is one of those places you would never find on your own. Truly secluded, it is an honour to be able to camp here. The ample paddock is slightly sloping, but most level around the edges. The sea view is not the most stunning but the environment is. It's so lovely here you can't help but be nice to each other.

| NA | 2 | NP | 5 | 0 AMP | | |

| £££ | | | M | | WiFi |

Directions: From Penzance take the A3315, signposted 'Porthcurno'. In 1 1/2 miles fork left, signposted 'Castallack'. At the right bend continue on to 'No through road' and at end bear left, site signed. Call at the farmhouse on the left.

GPS: N50°04.128'W005°33.259'
OS grid: 203 SW 458 247

June - September

56
Kenneggy Cove Holiday Park

Higher Kenneggy, Rosudgeon, Penzance, Cornwall TR20 9AU Tel: 01736 763453
www.kenneggycove.co.uk

Small and pleasant, this tranquil site has a policy of no noise after 10pm or before 8am. The tropical plants and landscaping create an attractive campsite during the season and a lovely garden when the site is closed. Sea views are available, but hedge growth could reduce this, although it does offer shelter from the wind. A 12 minute walk down a natural footpath brings you to the South West Coast Path and Kenneggy Sands, a stunning, secluded beach.

| NA | 4 | NP | 50 | 16 AMP | | |

| £££ | | | M | | WiFi |

Directions: The site is located halfway between Penzance and Helston off the A394. From the A30/A394 roundabout travel 4 miles east and turn right at the large blue 'Kenneggy Cove' sign. Follow the partly unmade road through farm buildings to the site. Access is tight in places.

GPS: N50°06.495'W005°24.735'
OS grid: 203 SW 562 286

Mid May - Mid October

57
Higher Pentreath Farm

Praa Sands, Penzance, Cornwall, TR20 9TL
Tel: 01736 763222

This site has not been ravaged by the modern world. Simple camping fields and basic facilities are all you need to enjoy this wonderful area. Stunning views are enjoyed from every camping field; the higher up you go the better the sea view and the quieter it gets. There is a 15 minute walk downhill to the beach.

| NA | 8 | NP | 100 | 10 AMP | |
| WC | | | | | |

Pub and beach 15 minutes downhill.

£££

Directions: Leave the A30 at the Penzance/Helston roundabout and take the A394 towards Helston. Go over the roundabout and through Rosudgeon. After the signpost for Newtown turn right into Pentreath Lane in front of Jet garage. The site is at the top of the hill.

GPS: N50°06.422'W005°23.692'
OS grid: 203 SW 574 284

March - October

59
Teneriffe Farm

Predannack, Mullion, Helston,
Cornwall TR12 7EZ
Tel: 01326 240293

This is a well cared for three acre site. Only five of the 24 pitches have a view of the sea, so pre-booking is advised. Mullion Cove is within easy walking distance as is Mullion, the largest village in Cornwall, which has numerous shops and pubs. Polurrian beach is 1 1/2 miles walk away, or you can drive five minutes to Polduh and 10 minutes to Kynannace beaches.

| NA | 3 | NP | 24 | 10 AMP | |
| WC | | | | | |

£££

Directions: 4 miles south of Helston turn right off the A3083 onto the B329. Travel 2 through Mullion towards Mullion Cove and turn left onto Ghost Hill, signposted 'Predannack'. The site is on the left in 1 1/4 miles.

GPS: N50°00.290'W005°14.968'
OS grid: 203 SW 672 166

March - October

Chycarne Holiday Park 60

Kuggar, Ruan Minor, Helston, Cornwall,
TR12 7LX Tel: 01326 290200
www.camping-cornwall.com

A mix of chalets, mobile homes, and camping facilities set within a sheltered, tree lined site combine to provide a safe, friendly and relaxing base from which to explore. Half the touring pitches on this pleasant site have views of the sea. The site is quiet and comfortable with great stargazing at night.

NA 8	NP 100	16 AMP		
WC				

Pub: Kennack Sands Inn. Beach 5 minutes.

££

Directions: Travelling towards Lizard Point on the A3083, turn left where signposted 'Kenneck Sands'. Travel one mile and turn left at the crossroads, again for 'Kenneck Sands'. Follow the road for one mile and the site is on the left once you enter Kuggar.

AA
▶▶▶

GPS: N50°00.258'W005°10.575'
OS grid: 204 SW 725 164

April - October

Trewince Farm 63

Portscatho, Truro, Cornwall TR2 5ET
Tel: 01872 580430
www.trewincefarm.co.uk

This five acre campsite is part of a working farm. The site owners are charming and the site is lovely. This ground is sloping, but there are many level pitches. Virtually every pitch offers views of the sea and those with obscured sea views have fantastic countryside views. Postscartho is a pretty Cornish village just two miles away, with a sandy beach, slipway, pubs and restaurants. Towan Beach is within walking distance.

NA 5	NP 25	13 AMP		
WC				

Pub and shop 1 mile at Gorran.

££

Directions: Good access for RVs. From St Austell take the A390 towards Truro. Bear left on the B3287 to Tregony. From Tregony follow the signs to St Mawes for seven miles to Trewithian and then turn left at the sign for Gerrans, Portscatho, Trewince Manor. Stay on this road, following signs for St Anthony to Trewince Farm half a mile beyond Gerrans village.

AA
▶▶▶

GPS: N50°09.965'W004°59.327'
OS grid: 204 SW 866 339

May - September

Seaview International Holiday Park | 65

Boswinger, Gorran, St Austell, Cornwall,
PL26 6LL Tel: 01726 843425
www.seaviewinternational.com

This is an exceptional campsite with excellent facilities and fully deserving of its five star status. Of the 189 touring pitches, only seven have a good view of the sea, so advanced booking is necessary. The sea can also be seen from the pool and children's play area. The beach is about a 10 minute walk down a narrow road or a five minute drive.

NA 27   NP 189   16 AMP

Beach 10 minute walk.

£££

Directions: Travelling between Mevagissi and Pentewan on the B3273, turn off and follow signs for Lost Gardens of Heligan. Continue past Heligan and site is four miles further on. Avoid Mevagissi town centre as it is narrow.

GPS: N50°14.219'W004°49.195'
OS grid: 204 SW 990 411

May - September

Treveague Farm Campsite | 66

Gorran, St Austell, Cornwall PL26 6NY
Tel: 01726-842295
http://treveaguefarm.co.uk

Treveague is a family run, 200 acre, organic working farm, breeding sheep, cattle, and pigs. The four acre, partly level campsite is on the brow of a hill. All pitches provide panoramic views across the rolling countryside and sea. There are two well appointed cottages for hire and all guests are encouraged to interact with the farm animals and watch the wildlife from special hides.

NA 200   NP 40   16 AMP

Pub and shop 1 mile at Gorran Haven.

£££

Directions: From St Austell follow B3273, turning off at signpost for 'Lost Gardens of Helligan'. Follow road past Lost Gardens and then follow signposts to 'Treveague Farm'.

GPS: N50°14.126'W004°48.169'
OS grid: 204 SX 004 413

April - October

67 Pentewan Sands Holiday Park

Pentewan, Cornwall, PL26 6BT
Tel: 01726 843485
www.pentewan.co.uk

This large commercial site has everything including its own private sandy beach. The site is mainly level, so only the front row has excellent sea views, however from theses 48 pitches you can literally roll out of bed and onto the beach, where there is a children's playground and designated swimming and boat areas. Pentewan village is two minutes walk away and the Lost Gardens of Helegan are two miles uphill. Advance booking is essential in high season when pitches are available for weekly slots only.

| NA 32 | NP 350 | 16 AMP |

Pub, shop, beach, slipway, play area and footpath onsite.

£££

Directions: From St Austell take the B3273. The site is adjacent to this road at Pentewan.

GPS: N50°17.289'W004°47.150'
OS grid: 204 SX 016 468

April - October

69 West Wayland Touring Park

West Wayland, Looe, Cornwall, PL13 2JS
Tel: 01503 262418
www.westwayland.co.uk

This is a beautifully kept campsite adjacent to the family farm. The grass is well maintained and unusually level. Most pitches offer views across the countryside to the sea. The owners take great pride in the site and the low tariff represents excellent value for money. There is a beach about one mile away and the pretty seaside town of Looe, with numerous shops, restaurants, pubs and a sandy beach is also close by.

| NA 20 | NP 120 | 16 AMP |

Pub and shop at Looe.

£££

Directions: Adacent to the A387 in between Looe and Polperro.

GPS: N50°21.117'W004°29.955'
OS grid: 201 SX 223 533

Easter - October

WEST OF ENGLAND

Bay View Farm [70]
Camping and Caravan Site

St Martins, Looe, Cornwall, PL13 1NZ
Tel: 01503 265922/07967 267312
www.looebaycaravans.co.uk

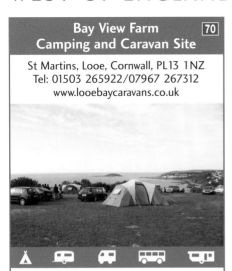

Two things make this site exceptional. First, the view is captivating. The site's elevated position overlooking Looe bay allows you to watch the comings and goings of fishing boats, and to enjoy the reflection of the town lights on the water at night. Second, Mike, the owner, has a friendly, laid back approach, which creates a very special atmosphere enhanced by his friendly shire horses grazing in adjacent paddocks. You can walk down to the beach or to Looe on the coast path. Looe is famed for its same day caught, daily fish market but it is also a pretty seaside town with pubs, restaurants and a sandy beach. Fishermen love it here as many charter boats offer everything from mackerel to shark fishing trips.

Pub, shop, beach and slipway at Looe.

Directions: Leave the A38 at Trerulefoot, seven miles west of Plymouth and take the A374 for one mile. Turn right onto the A387 towards Looe. At Widegates take the B3253 to Looe then turn left, after one mile, at No Mans Land. Follow signs to the Monkey Sanctuary. At the entrance to the Monkey Sanctuary bear right. About half a mile down, the lane ends and the site is on the right.

GPS: N50°21.839'W004°25.777'
OS grid: 201 SX 274 545

All Year

Mollie Tuckers Field CL [71]

East Prawle, Kingsbridge, Devon TQ7 2DF
Enq to; Wincot, Town Road, East Prawle, TQ7 2DF
Tel: 01548 511422 www.caravanclub.co.uk

This CL is just 50 metres from the village green where there are two pubs, a shop, and a café, and Stephens Field is also just around the corner. This is a buzzing place during the summer holidays with an August regatta, so you will need to pre book. Out of season you will be able to relax in peace and quiet and enjoy the wide open sea view.

Pub and shop 50 metres. Beach and slipway 20 minutes.

Directions: Drive straight through East Prawle village, signposted 'Prawle Point'. Mollies Field is on left through a five bar gate, signed.

GPS: N50°12.871'W003°42.596'
OS grid: 202 SX 780 362

All Year

Stephens Field [72]

East Prawle, Kingsbridge, Devon TQ7 2DF
Enq to; Wincot, Town Road, East Prawle, TQ7 2DF
Tel: 01548 511422 www.caravanclub.co.uk

This summer only camping field has a good sea view,
not quite as good as Mollie Tuckers Field which is
almost adjacent, but this site will probably be the
quietest when things are in full swing and is more
sheltered from the southwest. There are public toilets
by the adjacent village green as well as two pubs, a
shop, and a café.

| NA | 4 | NP | 25 | | | |
| WC | | | | | MG | MB |

Beach and slipway 20 minutes downhill.

£££

Directions: Drive straight through East Prawle village,
signposted 'Prawle Point'. Stephens Field is located at
the back left-hand side of the village green, down an
unmade road on the left and through a five bar gate,
signed 'Stephens Field'. Booking not necessary.

GPS: N50°12.883'W003°42.593'
OS grid: 202 SX 780 362

Summer Only

Slapton Sands Camping and Caravanning Site [73]

Middle Grounds, Slapton, Kingsbridge,
Devon TQ7 2QW Tel: 01548 580538
www.siteseeker.co.uk

Hedges and trees obscure what might otherwise be an
awesome view of the long shingle beach and the
amazing Slapton Ley, a long strip of fresh water just
behind the beach. Eight of the 25 pitches are set aside
for tourers. There are sandy beaches at each end of
the bay. From the site, the beach is a 20 minute
downhill walk on tarmac, or a five minute drive.

| NA | 3 | NP | 115 | 16 AMP | | |
| WC | | | | | MG | MB |

Pub 5 minutes. Shop and slipway at Torcross.

£££

Directions: Travelling along the A379 between the sea
and Slapton Ley (inland lake) turn inland by a
memorial, signed 'Caravaning quarter of a mile'. Follow
road uphill for a quarter of a mile and the
site is on the right, signposted 'Slapton'.

GPS: N50°17.439'W003°39.026'
OS grid: 202 SX 825 450

April - October

Hillhead Caravan Club Site [75]

Hillhead, Brixham, TQ5 0HH
Tel: 01803 853204
www.caravanclub.co.uk

Few pitches have a view of the sea, but this is an exceptional site. Hedged terraced areas create a secluded feel. Many of the pitches are serviced hard standings. The communal facilities are second to none and there is a great children's castellated play area. Mansands Beach is a vigorous 2¹/2 mile downhill walk.

| NA | 22 | NP | 239 | 16 AMP | | |
| WC | | | | | | MG |

Beach 15 minutes downhill.

£££

Directions: At Hillhead turn off the A379 onto B3205, signposted 'Kingswear', 'Dartmouth', and' Lower Ferry'. Follow the road for 220m and the site is on the left, clearly signed.

GPS: N50°22.207'W003°32.696'
OS grid: 202 SX 904 534

March - January

Beverley Park Caravan & Camping Site [77]

Goodrington Road, Paignton, Devon,
TQ4 7JE Tel: 01803 843887
www.beverley-holidays.co.uk

This is a family orientated holiday complex with lots of excellent facilities and plenty of static caravans for hire. There are plenty of camping pitches but the area with the best sea views is gently sloping. The Top Bar has an outside terrace overlooking the large heated outdoor pool, camping fields onto the sea and the English Riviera. Everywhere is very well kept and clean.

| NA | 20 | NP | 180 | 16 AMP | | |
| WC | | | | | | |

£££

Directions: From the A385/A380/A3022 'Threeways Cross', head south on the A3022 towards Brixham. Travel one mile and, at the traffic lights, turn left into Goodrington Road. Follow the road uphill and Beverly Park is signposted on the left in half a mile.

GPS: N50°24.828'W003°34.117'
OS grid: 202 SX 886 582

All Year

Coast View

78

Torquay Road, Shaldon, Teignmouth,
South Devon, TQ14 0BG
Tel: 01626 872392 www.coastview.co.uk

Many unfolding layers await you at this unique site. The awesome panoramic sea view from the top tent field is probably the widest in the country. You enter the site right in the heart of the busy entertainment area. As you climb the steep road, you pass excellent chalets and static caravans, then on to the well laid out, level touring pitches, past the camping terraces and higher up to the large, informal camping fields where you should be able to pitch far from your neighbours and the excellent facilities.

NA 17   NP 115   10 AMP

Pub, shop and beach 1 mile at Shaldon.

£££

Directions: Be aware of grounding on entering/exiting site. Adjacent to the A379 as you exit Shaldon towards Torquay.

GPS: N50°32.104'W003°30.163'
OS grid: 203 SX 935 717

March - October

Ladram Bay Caravan Site

79

Otterton, Budleigh Salterton, Devon,
EX9 7BX Tel: 01395 568398
www.ladrambay.co.uk

This is a one stop holiday spot. Remotely located, this is a big site with lots of quality accommodation and excellent facilities. You could come here for a week and feel no need to leave site. The private shingle beach is just stunning and there is a slipway to the beach with boat storage adjacent. The terraced camping fields have fantastic sea views from most pitches. Indeed sea views can be seen from most places, but the bar terrace has the best. There is a very well stocked shop, fantastic children's entertainment ,and it is directly on the coast path.

NA 20   NP 200   16 AMP

£££

Directions: Turn off the B3052 onto the B3178, signposted 'Budleigh Salterton'. Turn off where signposted 'Ladram Bay' and 'Camping'. Follow signposts to Ladram Bay.

GPS: N50°39.709'W003°17.136'
OS grid: 192 SY 096 851

April - October

Salcombe Regis Camping and Caravan Park

[80]

Salcombe Regis, Sidmouth, Devon,
EX10 0JH Tel: 01395 514303
www.salcombe-regis.co.uk

This is a gorgeous, medium sized site that really offers quality camping in every aspect. Unfortunately, only a handful of tent pitches benefit from the wonderful valley and sea view. The park and its facilities are kept immaculately. Sidmouth, about 10 minutes drive away, retains its Regency and Victorian elegance, and boasts two pebble beaches which, at low tide, give way to golden sand and rock pools.

| NA | 16 | NP | | 16 AMP | | |

£££

Directions: The park is well signposted on the Exeter-Lyme Regis road (A3052), from both directions. Do not take your caravan into Sidmouth itself. From the east, on the A3052, take the first turning left after the Donkey Sanctuary. Follow the road for half a mile and the campsite is on the left-hand side, just past the golf range.

GPS: N50°41.743'W003°12.307'
OS grid: 192 SY 149 892

Mid March - October

Golden Cap

[83]

Seatown, Chideock, Bridport, Dorset,
DT6 6JX Tel: 01308 422139
www.wdlh.co.uk

This site is located perfectly for a beach holiday as there is easy access to the shingle beach, which is only two minutes walk away. Unfortunately, only a handful of pitches have a good sea view and advanced booking is required. There are glimpses of the sea in some other areas, but there are good views of the surrounding hills almost everywhere. Pitches are well defined with plenty of shrubs and trees breaking up the site. Levelling blocks are supplied where required and some areas are a little cosy. A modern toilet block is provided.

| NA | 154 | NP | 159 | 10 AMP | | |

Pub 100 metres. Slipway 2 miles.

£££

Directions: Take the A35 to Chideock. Turn off, opposite the church into Duck Street, for Seatown. Follow this road to the coast and the park entrance is on the left, just before the car park.
Note: This is a narrow lane.

GPS: N50°43.415'W002°49.325'
OS grid: 193 SY 423 920

March - October

Highlands End Holiday Park `84`

Eype, Bridport, Dorset, DT6 6AR
Tel: 01308 422139
www.wdlh.co.uk

The camping fields of this site offer exceptional views, some over rolling hills, some over the cliffs to the sea. This site oozes quality and refinement that you can sense as you come down the drive. The bar has wonderful old Royal Berkshire fire engines on display and there is also a large, formal restaurant. The Heritage Coastline offers wonderful walking and it is just 500 metres downhill to the shingle beach.

NA	27	NP	192	10 AMP		
WC					MG	MB

Pub, shop and beach at West Bay.

£££

Directions: Southwest of Bridport, turn off the A35, signposted 'Eype'. Follow this road and take the fourth right turning to the site entrance, clearly signposted and follow the road to reception.

GPS: N50°43.263'W002°46.634'
OS grid: 193 SY 452 913

March - October

Eype House Caravan Park `85`

Eype, Bridport, Dorset DT6 6AL
Tel: 01308 424903
www.eypehouse.co.uk

Approached down a very narrow, high-hedged lane, this lovely south facing, steeply sloping, terraced site is only suitable for tents and small campervans. The elevated location provides excellent views from every pitch, down to the beach and along a section of the Jurassic coast. There are static caravans for hire below the tent pitches. The pebble beach is a 200m downhill walk with 14 steps along the path.

NA	4	NP	20	0 AMP		
WC					MG	MB

Pub, shop, beach and slipway at West Bay.

£££

Directions: This site is not licensed for touring caravans. 1 1/4 miles West of Bridport on the A35. Take the turning south to Eype and drive through the village towards the sea.

GPS: N50°43.045'W002°47.043'
OS grid: 193 SY 446 912

All Year

Windridge CL [88]

481 Chickerell Road, Weymouth, Dorset,
DT3 4DQ Tel: 01305 779268
www.caravanclub.co.uk

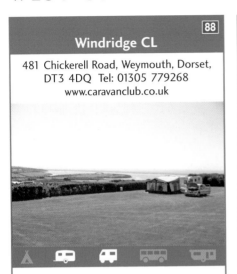

This five van site really pulls it out of the bag. It is an island of tranquillity with views in all directions, and looking out to sea across Chesil Beach is blissful. Although the site is flanked on one side by a waste transfer site and the other by an MOD firing range, this does not detract from the site which is popular, so advanced booking is required.

NA 2   NP 5

Pub, shop and beach at Weymouth.

£££   M

Directions: Two miles from Weymouth town centre. In between Chickerell and Weymouth at a bungalow between the Hansen facility and the WRTA rifle range on the B3157. Pull off into a small lane beside a brick bungalow, which will be on your left if you're heading north on Chickerell Road. Not clearly signed, but less than a quarter of a mile past Fleet Lane heading north on the B3157.

GPS: N50°36.976'W002°30.063'
OS grid: 194 SY 646 797

All Year

Pebble Bank [90]

90 Camp Road, Wyke Regis, Weymouth,
Dorset, DT4 9HF Tel: 01305 774844
www.pebblebank.co.uk

Ajacent to Chesil Beach, this is a homely and comfortable site. There are 100 static caravans, both privately owned and rented. Tourers have their own small, pine tree edged, partly sloping area overlooking the fleet, fisherman's huts, and Chesil Beach. Access to the fleet is 100m. The one acre tent field at the top of the site has spectacular views across Portland and Chesil Beach.

NA 5   NP 40   10 AMP

WC

Pub and shop at Old Wyke.

£££   M

Directions: Travelling on the A354 through Weymouth towards Portland, turn right at the roundabout by the Rodwell pub into Wyke Road. Travel one straight mile and at the right-hand bend, just past the church, carry straight on into Camp Road. The site is on the left in 500 yards.

GPS: N50°35.774'W002°29.248'
OS grid: 194 SY 657 776

March - October

Durdle Door Holiday Park

92

Lulworth Cove, Wareham, Dorset, BH20 5PU
Tel: 01929 400200
www.lulworth.com

This is one of the few places on this section of coast where there is access to the sea, and many day visitors take advantage of this. There are plenty of non sea view pitches, including a very pleasant area under pine trees which is ideal during hot spells. A single row of pitches set back from the cliff provides the few sea view pitches available. However, most of these are so steep that only touring caravans can level by perching on concrete blocks. Unfortunately, day parking spoils the tranquillity and attractive views.

NA 45   NP 108   ☠ 16 AMP

WC   ♿   🔥   🛁   📷   MG

🚰   🧺   🔍   ⚓   🚣   🅰   🚶

Slipway 1 mile at Lulworth Cove.

£££   🐕   👫   M   ⓘ   WiFi

Directions: On the A31 past Ringwood to Bere Regis. From Bere Regis follow local signs to Wool, then take the B3071 to West Lulworth. Continue past The Castle Inn and the war memorial then, taking the first right, continue past the church and up the hill. The entrance to Durdle Door Holiday Park is on the brow of the hill, on the left.

GPS: N50°37.612'W002°16.096'
OS grid: 194 SY 812 809

March - October

Slimeridge Farm Touring Park   **1**
Links Road, Uphill, Weston-Super-Mare, Somerset, BS23 4XY
Tel: 01934 641641
Leave the M5 motorway at Junction 22, and drive north onto the A38 towards Bristol. Fork left onto the A370 road towards Weston-Super-Mare, turning left at Weston Hospital, Grange Road. Continue and turn right at the roundabout. Take the first road left, Uphill Way, towards the beach and follow the signs to the site which is adjacent to Weston-Super-Mare beach.

Home Farm Holiday Centre   **3**
St Audries Bay, Williton, Somerset, TA4 4DP
Tel: 01984 632487
www.homefarmholidaycentre.co.uk
Travelling south on the M5, exit at Junction 24 and take the A39 towards Minehead for 17 miles to West Quantoxhead. After passing St Audries Garage on the left, take the first right, B3191, signposted 'Blue Anchor Bay' and 'Doniford'. The site entrance is half a mile on the right-hand side. The site road is long and has several traffic humps.

St Audries Bay Holiday Club   **4**
West Quantoxhead, Near Minehead, Somerset, TA4 4DY
Tel: 01984 632515
www.staudriesbay.co.uk
From the north on the M5, leave the motorway at Junction 24 and take the A39 towards Minehead for 15 miles towards West Quantoxhead. The site entrance is on your right just before the village.

Mullacott Farm   **16**
Ilfracombe, North Devon, EX34 8NA
Tel: 01271 866877
www.mullacottfarm.co.uk
Take the A361 from Barnstaple to Ilfracombe. Pass over the cross-roads where the B3343 bisects the A361, and the site is about half a mile on your left.

Woolacombe Sands Holiday Park   **17**
Beach Road, Woolacombe, Devon, EX34 7AF
N51°10.300'W004°11.433'   Tel: 01271 870569
www.woolacombe-sands.co.uk
From Barnstaple, travel 10 miles towards Ilfracombe on the A316. At the Mullacott Cross roundabout, turn left onto the B3343 towards Woolacombe and follow the named campsite signs.

Mitchums and Myrtle Campsite `22`
Moor Lane, Croyde, Devon, EX33 1NN
Tel: 07891 892897
www.croydebay.co.uk
From Braunton, take the B3231 to Croyde. From Croyde village take Moor Lane. Tents Only.

Twitchen House `24`
Mortehoe, Woolacombe, Devon, EX34 7ES
Tel: 01271 870343
www.woolacombe.com
From Barnstaple, travel 10 miles toward Ilfracombe on the A316. At the Mullacott Cross roundabout turn left onto the B3343 towards Woolacombe. In 1.7 miles turn right, signed Mortehoe and campsite name into Mortehoe Station Rd. Travel 1.4 miles and the site entrance is on the left, clearly signed.

Braddicks Holiday Centre `25`
Merely Road, Westward-Ho, North Devon, EX39 1JU
Tel: 01237 473263
www.braddicksholidaycentre.co.uk
Enter Westward-Ho from the B3236 and turn left, or west, along the sea front and the site is on the right overlooking the sea.

Wooda Farm Park `28`
Poughill, Bude, Cornwall. EX23 9HJ
Tel: 01288 352069
www.wooda.co.uk
Turn left off the A39 Wadebridge to Bideford road on the outskirts of Stratton, at the signpost to Poughill and Coombe Valley. The site is on the right in three quarters of a mile.

Penstowe Caravan and Camping Park `29`
Kilkhampton, near Bude, Cornwall, EX23 9QY
Tel: 01288 321354 / 08448 471356
www.hoseasons.co.uk
North of Bude on the A39, turn left, travelling north to Sandymouth and the site is 200 yards on the right.

Bude Camping and Caravanning Club Site `31`
Gillards Moor, St Gennys, Bude, Cornwall, EX23 0BG
Tel: 01840 230650
www.campingandcaravanningclub.co.uk
From the north on A39, the site is on the right in a lay-by nine miles from Bude.

Higher Harlyn Park `37`
St Merryn, Padstow, Cornwall, PL28 8SG
Tel: 01841 520022
www.higherharlynpark.co.uk
Travelling south on the A39, pass Wadebridge and in five miles turn right at the roundabout onto the B3274, signed 'Padstow'. Travel three miles and turn left at the crossroads to St Merryn, then travel three more miles to St Merryn centre. At the crossroads, go straight over and the site is on the left in half a mile, clearly signed.

Atlantic View `39`
Trevemedar Farm, St Eval, Wadebridge, Cornwall, PL27 7UT
Tel: 01841 520431
On the B3276, Padstow to Newquay. $3^1/_2$ miles from St Merryn and three quarters of a mile south of Porthcothan.

Trevornick Holiday Park `42`
Holywell Bay, Newquay, Cornwall, TR8 5PW
Tel: 01637 830531 / 0845 3455531
www.trevornick.co.uk
Three miles south of Newquay on the A3075, on Redruth Road. Turn northwest to Cubert and Holywell Bay.

Watergate Bay Touring Park `43`
Newquay, Cornwall, TR8 4AD
Tel: 01637 860387
www.watergatebaytouringpark.eclipse.co.uk
14 miles west of Bodmin on the A30. Turn right after the railway bridge and follow the signposts for the airport to the B3276. The site is in half a mile on the left of this junction.

St Ives Bay Holiday Park `49`
Upton Towans, Hayle, Cornwall, TR27 5BH
Tel: 01736 752274 / 0800 317713
www.stivesbay.co.uk
Take the M5 southwest at Bristol, then change to the A30, signposted 'Okehampton', after Exeter services. Stay on the A30 until the last half mile of your journey. You will bypass Okehampton, Launceston, Bodmin, Redruth and Camborne. After Camborne the road goes through a big dip. At the bottom of the next hill take the Hayle exit and then turn right at the mini roundabout, signed for campsite, and follow the road for approximately half a mile. The park is on the left, clearly signed.

Bosverbas 58

Germoe, Near Praa Sands, Penzance, Cornwall.
TR20 9AA
Tel: 01736 762277
East on the A394 road towards Ashton and Helston.
After the Jet Garage at Newtown, in 150 yards, turn
north onto a private road for 100 yards.

Gwendreath Farm Caravan Park 61

Ruan Minor, Helston, Cornwall,
TR12 7LZ.
Tel: 01326 290666
www.tomandlinda.co.uk
Approaching from Helston on the B3293, pass the
Satellite Earth Station on your right and turn right at
the crossroads, signposted 'Kennack Sands' and
'Cadgwith'. Turn left in 1 1/2 miles, signposted
'Gwendreath', and look for the sign for 'Gwendreath
Farm Holiday Park'.

Porthkerris Cove 62

St Keverne, Cornwall, TR12 6QJ
Tel: 01326 280620
www.porthkerris.co.uk
From St Keverne, turn left into the square, keeping the
White Hart pub on your left. Then turn left out of St
Keverne, past the fire station on your left. Follow the
road towards Porthallow, past some gates with stone
eagles on your right, then take the next right, and then
the next left, following the signs to Porthkerris Dive
Centre. The road is very narrow, so campervans only.

Arthurs Field 64

Treloan Coastal Farm, Treloan Lane, Portscatho,
The Roseland, Truro, Cornwall, TR2 5EF
Tel: 01872 580989
Take the A30 from Exeter to Okehampton and then the
A3076 to Truro. Approximately five miles past Trispen,
turn left where signposted 'A390 to St Austell', through
Tresillian and onto the Probus Bypass. Take the second
turning onto the A3078, signposted 'Tregony' and 'St
Mawes'. Approximately seven miles past Tregony to
Trewithian turn left, signposted 'Portscatho' and
'Gerrans' to Church. Take Treloan Lane and the site is
300 yards on the left.

Penhale Caravan and Camping Park 68

Fowey, Cornwall, PL23 1JU.
Tel: 01726 833425
www.penhale-fowey.co.uk
1 1/2 miles southwest of Lostwithiel on the A390 St
Austell Road, turn southeast on the B3269, signposted
'Fowey'. Continue to the roundabout one mile from
Fowey, then turn right onto the A3082 Par road. The
site is on the left in half a mile.

Dartmouth Caravan and Camping Club 74

Dartmouth Road, Stoke Fleming, Dartmouth, Devon,
TQ6 0RF
Tel: 01803 770253
www.campingandcaravanningclub.co.uk
The site is located two miles south of Dartmouth on the
A379, half a mile north of Stoke Fleming.

Leonards Cove 76

Dartmouth, South Devon, TQ6 0NR
Tel: 01803 770206
www.leonardscove.co.uk
From the M5 take the A38, signposted 'Plymouth'.
Leave the A38 at Buckfastleigh onto the A384 Totnes.
Turn right at the traffic lights in Totnes, onto the A381
to Kingsbridge. At Halwell, turn left onto the A3122 to
Dartmouth. From Dartmouth, take the A379 to Stoke
Fleming. The entrance to Leonards Cove is in the middle
of the village on the left.

Manor Farm Caravan Site 81

Seaton Down Road, Seaton, Devon, EX12 2JA
Tel: 01297 21524
www.manorfarmcaravansite.com
Seven miles west of Lyme Regis on the A3052 Seaton
road. Turn left at the Tower Filling Station. One mile
north of Seaton.

Seadown Holiday Park 82

Bridge Road, Charmouth, Dorset, DT6 6QS
Tel: 01297 560154
www.seadownholidaypark.co.uk
From the east, take the turning off the Bridport-
Axminster A35 road for Charmouth. In half a mile turn
left into Bridge Road. The site entrance is 100 yards
directly in front. From the west, at the roundabout west
of Charmouth, DO NOT go into Charmouth but
continue on the by-pass for three quarters of a mile and
follow the directions as above.

WEST OF ENGLAND

West Bay Holiday Park `86`
West Bay, Bridport, Dorset, DT6 4HB
Tel: 01308 459491
www.parkdeanholidays.co.uk
From Dorchester take the A35 to Bridport. At the first
roundabout take first exit, and at the second
roundabout take the second exit into West Bay. The
park is on the right.

Bagwell Farm Touring Park `87`
Bagwell Farm, Chickerell, Weymouth, Dorset, DT3 4EA
Tel: 01305 782575
www.bagwellfarm.co.uk
In Weymouth, turn west on the B3157 road to
Chickerell. Continue northwest for three miles, past the
Victoria Inn. Turn left to the site.

Littlesea Holiday Park `89`
Lynch Lane, Weymouth, Dorset, DT4 9DT
Tel: 01305 774414
www.havenholidays.com
From Weymouth drive west on the B3157 towards
Chickerell. Just before Granby Industrial Estate turn
south and take the first turning right to Lynch Lane.
The site is at the end of the lane.

East Fleet Farm Touring Park `91`
Fleet Lane, Chickerell, Weymouth, Dorset, DT3 4DW
Tel: 01305 785768
www.eastfleet.co.uk
Three miles west of Weymouth on the B3157 Bridport
road. Turn left at the brown camp site sign, down Fleet
Lane for half a mile to the site.

Cliff Farm CL `93`
Aust, Bristol, Gloucester, BS35 4BG
Tel: 01454 632400
www.caravanclub.co.uk
Leave the M48 at Junction one onto the A403
Avonmouth road. In 100 yards turn right across the
dual carriageway. In about 150 yards past a CL on the
left, turn right over a cattle grid into the drive. The site
entrance to Cliff Farm is at the end.

Ladram Bay Beach

Southwold Beach Huts

Folkestone, Kent

ENGLAND

Warden Springs Holiday Park

PRAWNS
1 PINT
£1.50

OFFER
2 PINTS
£2.50

ENGLAND

Aldeburgh Beach Crab Sellers

Beeston Regis Beach

ENGLAND

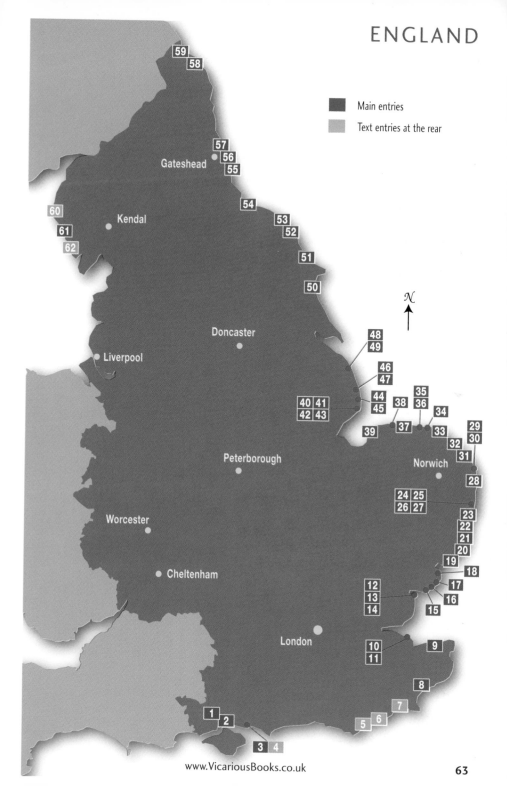

ENGLAND

Main entries

Text entries at the rear

59
58

57
56
55
Gateshead

54
53
52
60
61 Kendal
62

51

50

N

Doncaster
48
49
Liverpool
46
47
44 35
40 41 38 36
42 43 45 34
39 37 33 29
32 30
31
Peterborough Norwich
28

24 25
26 27
23
Worcester 22
21
20
19
Cheltenham 18
17
12 16
13 15
14

10 9
London 11

8

7

1 5 6
2

3 4

ENGLAND

Stonehill Farm CL

Calshot Road, Fawley, Southampton,
SO45 1DW Tel: 02380 891442
www.caravanclub.co.uk

© Russ and Mandy Valentine

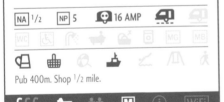

Homely and quiet, this is a level site with five small camping bays. There are fascinating views over Southampton Water and all the busy traffic that sails through it.

NA 1/2   NP 5   16 AMP

Pub 400m. Shop 1/2 mile.

£££   M   WiFi

Directions: Leave the M27 at Junction 2 onto the A326, signposted 'Fawley'. Travel 11 miles, to the end of the A326 and turn left onto the B3053, signposted 'Calshot Activity Centre'. Within 1 3/4 miles, 100 yards past the left turn to Ashlett, turn left into a track, signposted 'Stonehill Farm'. The site is on the left at the end of the track.

GPS: N50°49.370'W001°20.543'
OS grid: 196 SU 464 028

All Year

2

Arden CL

Arden, Occupation Lane, Fareham,
Hampshire, P014 4BZ Tel: 01329 845199
www.caravanclub.co.uk

© Graham Burrows

Arden CL is situated on relatively flat grounds, one mile west of the historic village of Titchfield. The site is quiet and peaceful and has views over fields to the Solent and the busy waterways to Southampton and Portsmouth. There is direct access to footpaths that lead to the Solent, a sand/shingle beach, Meon River and the Titchfield Bird Haven. This location is close to the ferry port of Portsmouth for onward travel, or return, to France and Spain.

NA 3/4   NP 5   16 AMP

£££   M   WiFi

Directions: Leave the M27 at Junction 9 onto the A27 Fareham-Portsmouth road. In 1 1/2 miles, at the second roundabout, turn right into St Margaret's Lane. At the T-junction turn left into Coach Hill, signposted 'Titchfield/Fareham'. Then immediately turn right into Posbrook Lane, signposted 'Meon'. In 600 yards, turn right into a track, signposted 'Arden'. Continue through the automatic gate, into the site. Set Sat Nav to PO14 4EZ - Posbrook Lane.

GPS: N50°50.525'W001°14.517'
OS grid: 196 SU 532 052

All Year

Fishery Creek Caravan and Camping Park [3]

100 Fishery Lane, Hayling Island, Hampshire,
PO11 9NR Tel: 02392 462164
www.keyparks.co.uk

Library Picture

The park is set in a beautiful and quiet location adjoining a tidal creek that flows to Chichester Harbour. If you book a creekside pitch, you will be able to watch the ebb and flow of the tidal waters or fish from the bankside. There are modern toilet blocks and the site is well laid out with tarmac roads and attractive flowers and shrubs. A five minute walk takes you to an old fashioned seafront with a pebbly beach, local shops, restaurants, pubs and clubs.

| NA | 4 | NP | 90 | ☠ | 10 AMP | | |

Pub and shop 5 minutes.

£££

Directions: From the A27 take the A3023, signed 'Hayling Island'. At the first roundabout turn left and follow the brown signs to Fishery Creek Park.

GPS: N50°47.055'W000°57.530'
OS grid: 197 SZ 733 987

March - October

Folkestone Camping and Caravanning Club Site [8]

The Warren, Folkestone, Kent, CT19 6NQ
Tel: 01303 255093
www.siteseeker.co.uk

This narrow site is set into the side of the white cliffs of Dover adjacent to a quiet sandy beach. Pitches are well distributed in small groups and some have excellent sea views. The local area bears witness to its military past with opportunities for walking and fishing along the concrete sea defences. Folkestone is a 25 minute hilly walk away. The overgrown private access road has cars parked on it all day, often making access very difficult.

| NA | 4 | NP | 80 | ☠ | 16 AMP | | |

Pub, shop and slipway at Folkestone.

£££

Directions: From the A2 or A20, join the A260 and follow the signs to the Country Park. At the roundabout follow Hill Road. At the cross roads, drive into Wear Bay Road signposted, 'Martello Tower'. The site is the fifth on the left just as you can see the sea.

GPS: N51°05.622'E001°12.372'
OS grid: 179 TR 246 376

March - October

ENGLAND

Seaview Holiday Park [9]

St John's Road, Swalecliffe, Nr Whitstable,
Kent, CT5 2RY Tel: 0845 8159755
www.parkholidaysuk.com/seaview

This site occupies an enviable beachside location halfway between fashionable Whitstable and traditional Herne Bay. The sea wall obscures nearly all the view from this level site and the touring field is behind a high hedge. A large rally field is adjacent to the seawall, so front row campers should have a good sea view. The beach can be nonexistent or vast depending on the tide. There is an outdoor pool and a large bar onsite, and outside the gate there are local shops and a pub. Insurance documents must be shown prior to using the onsite slipway.

| NA | 80 | NP | 171 | 10 AMP | | |

Pub and shop 5 minutes. Slipway £2.

£££

Directions: A299 Thanet Way and join the A2990 towards Swalecliffe. At the large Texaco roundabout, turn north driving under the railway bridge (4m, 13ft) and turn immediately right onto St Johns Road. The site is in half a mile on a sharp right hand bend, clearly signed.

GPS: N51°21.995'E001°04.609'
OS grid: 179 TR 142 675

March - October

Priory Hill Touring Park [10]

Wing Road, Leysdown, Isle of Sheppey,
Kent, ME12 4QT Tel: 01795 510267
www.prioryhill.co.uk

This small, comfortable touring site is located on the outskirts of Leysdown. The site is split in two by a quiet road. The statics, bar, and indoor pool are behind the two small touring fields which are set a short way back from the sea. There are views of the sea from just about every pitch. The field adjacent to the picnic area has the widest view over the coastal park to the sea beyond.

| NA | 2 | NP | 36 | 10 AMP | | |

Slipway behind Little Groves static park.

£££

Directions: Take the M20 from London to the A249, signposted to Sheerness. Then take the B2231 to Leysdown on Sea.

GPS: N51°23.692'E000°55.586'
OS grid: 178 TR 036 707

March - October

ENGLAND

Warden Springs Park Resorts [11]

Thorn Hill Road, Warden Point, Eastchurch, Isle of
Sheppey, Kent, ME12 4HF Tel: 0844 0502579
www.park-resorts.com/wardensprings

This site is perched on, fossil rich, mud cliffs offering
good views across the site but especially from the
touring field which is right on the edge of the cliffs.
Several pitches are set at right angles to the sea and
flanked by conifer trees. The site is in a remote
location so additional transport is beneficial, however
the beach is a 15 minute walk away and there is a bar,
outdoor pool and small shop onsite.

NA 3.5   NP 56   16 AMP

Beach 15 minutes walk. Slipway at Leysdown.

£££

Directions: In the centre of Eastchurch, turn north
beside the church and travel 650m taking the first
right into Warden Road. Follow this road for two miles
to the site road (Thorn Hill) and the site
is 200m on the left. Thorn Hill road
leads to Leysdown but may not be
suitable for accessing the site with large
vehicles.

★★★★
HOLIDAY PARK

GPS: N51°24.724'E000°54.037'
OS grid: 178 TR 017 721

Easter - October

Seaview Holiday Park [12]

Seaview Avenue, West Mersea, Essex,
CO5 8DA Tel: 01206 382534
www.holidayseaview.co.uk

This campsite has a traditional, nostalgic feel yet the
owners are investing for future generations. This 30
acre, partly wooded park slopes gently down to a private
beach, lined with rentable designer beach huts painted
in pleasing pastel colours. Unfortunately, the huts stop
all but five hard standing pitches from enjoying a sea
view. The toilet blocks are just far enough away to
encourage you to use your own facilities, but water and
emptying points are near to the pitches. The beach has
sand banks and shallow water, making it excellent for
windsurfing. The Mersea Windsurf Club is adjacent.

NA   NP 65   16 AMP

250 metres to showers.

£££

Directions: Travel onto Mersea Island. Take the left
fork to East Mersea on East Mersea Road, signposted
'Camping', and then travel half a mile and take the first
right onto Dawes Lane, signposted 'Seaview'. Travel to
the end and, at the crossroads, turn right, then first
left. Follow Seaview signs and the campsite is on the
left when you reach the sea.

GPS: N51°46.454'E000°55.983'
OS grid: 168 TM 024 124

Easter - October

13
Fen Farm

Moore Lane, East Mersea, Colchester,
Essex, CO5 8FE Tel: 01206 383275
www.fenfarm.co.uk

The majority of visitors to this site will camp on the two flat fields at the top of the site, from which there are limited views. Since 1918, this family run site has developed gently and now has 60 seasonal pitches and 80 private statics, many of which have wonderful marsh and sea views over a large expanse of south facing, tidal, sandy beach. The proximity of the Essex marshes and the presence of many birds and wildlife create a tranquil atmosphere.

| NA 8 | NP 80 | 10 AMP | | |
| WC | | | | MG | MB |

M/h waste in boat wash. Pub 5 mins. Slipway West Mersea.

£££ | | | M | (i) | WiFi

Directions: Travel onto Mersea Island. Take the left fork to East Mersea on East Mersea Road, signposted 'Camping', and then the fifth right in 2.8 miles signposted 'Fen Farm'.

GPS: N51°47.433'E000°59.042'
OS grid: 168 TM 058 144

March - October

14
Waldegraves

Waldgraves Lane, East Mersea Colchester,
Essex, CO5 8SE Tel: 01206 382898
www.waldegraves.co.uk

This park offers the most sea view touring pitches on the island. The onsite restaurant/bar/shop complex is attractive and businesslike, and the bar meals looked excellent value for money. The extensive touring field gently slopes toward the sea but has level areas and some trees and hedges. There are four well stocked fishing lakes, an eighteen hole golf course, an outdoor pool and a boating lake. The onsite slipway provides access to the sea approximately three hours either side of high tide. Buoyed zones segregate bathers from powered craft.

| NA 8 | NP 309 | 10 AMP | | |
| WC | | | | MG | MB |

Slipway onsite. Liftable manhole.

£££ | | | M | (i) | WiFi

Directions: Travel onto Mersea Island. Take the left fork to East Mersea on East Mersea Road, then in 1.6 miles take the second turning to the right, Chapmans Lane. Follow the brown and cream Tourist Board signs to Waldegraves.

GPS: N51°46.701'E000°56.881'
OS grid: 168 TM 035 128

March - November

15 Martello Beach Holiday Park

Belsize Avenue, Jaywick, Clacton-On-Sea,
Essex, CO15 2LF Tel: 01255 820060
www.park-resorts.com/holiday-parks/essex/martello-beach

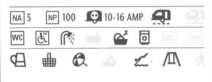

This family site is a stone's throw, over the sea wall, from seven miles of golden sandy beach. There are no views onsite. The local area has a unique, forgotten feel and Clacton, with its famous pier, is only a few miles drive away. Exhibitions, events, and workshops, are held in the local Martello Tower which has a floor to ceiling projection screen. The campsite has good children's facilities, including a pool complex and arcade. Pitches are un-hedged, flat, and a standard 6m by 6m, and some are shaded by the surrounding trees.

NA 5	NP 100	10-16 AMP

£££

Directions: Travel south on the A133 to the outskirts of Clacton. At St John's roundabout take the fourth exit (right) onto the B1077. Continue one mile, passing the garden centre, and turn left at the mini roundabout onto Jaywick Lane. Continue three miles until you reach Broadway, then follow the road signs to the site.

GPS: N51°46.391'E001°05.879'
OS grid: 169 TM 137 128

Easter - October

16 Naze Marine Holiday Park

Hall Lane, Walton-on-the-Naze, Essex,
CO14 8HL Tel: 01255 682410
www.park-resorts.com/holiday-parks/essex/naze-marine

Max 26ft

The site is set back from the coast, but it is an easy three minute walk along a quiet road takes you to the big, sandy beach, lined with beach huts. There are spectacular scenic views from the top of the ancient Naze Tower. Walton on the Naze is five minutes' walk; from here, you can charter a fishing boat or fish from the pier. The flat, open camping area has unbounded 6m by 6m pitches and are classed as standard (non-electric) and serviced (electric included). Longer stay touring pitches are also available. A modern Portacabin complex houses toilets and showers.

NA 46	NP 40	16 AMP

£££

Directions: Follow the A12 toward Colchester and exit at Junction 29 taking the A120, signposted, 'Harwich', until you reach the A133, signposted 'Weeley'. Take the A133 as far as Weeley. At the roundabout, take the first exit onto the B1033. Follow the B1033, then the B1336, then the B1304 all the way to Walton seafront. Turn left up Hall lane and Naze Marine Holiday Park is on the left in 500m.

GPS: N51°51.330'E001°16.706'
OS grid: 169 TM 257 224

Easter - October

ENGLAND

Dovercourt Caravan Park [17]

Low Road, Dovercourt, Essex, CO12 3TZ
Tel: 01255 243433
www.dovercourtcp.com

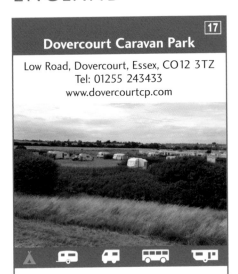

This is the perfect night halt site when travelling to Holland and discounts are given to Stena Line ticket holders. Reception does not take advanced bookings, but you are always likely to get a pitch. Several hedges break up the camping area so you can often have your own space. The camping field is in the far corner of the park, 100m from the sea, but has no view due to the sea defence. Site roads are narrow and bendy and big vehicles will scrub tyres along the curbs in places. There is a coastal path to the marsh and Dovercourt beach with its historic iron lighthouses.

| NA | 15 | NP | 60 | 16 AMP |

Dovercourt beach 7 - 10 minutes.

£££

Directions: Travelling east, follow the A120 to Ramsey Roundabout and turn right onto the B1352. In approximately one mile turn right at the mini roundabout by the Devon Public House. Turn left at the next mini roundabout, which takes you onto Low Road. Dovercourt Caravan Park is about a mile on the right.

GPS: N51°55.577'E001°15.535'
OS grid: 169 TM 241 229

April - October

Peewit Caravan Park [18]

Walton Avenue, Felixstowe, Suffolk, IP11 2HB
Tel: 01394 284511
www.peewitcaravanpark.co.uk

This privately owned, quiet, and secluded campsite is set in 13 acres of tree lined and landscaped parkland. It is a pleasantly traditional site with an atmosphere of tranquillity. Onsite there is an aviary with seats and a water feature. There is also a small fenced play area for the under fives. There are no sea views from site, but then there are no campsites for miles with a sea view, so the 900m, flat walk to Felixstowe's four miles of mixed sand/shale beach is very short in comparison. There is a traditional seafront with beach huts and promenade.

| NA | 13 | NP | 65 | 10-16 AMP |

Children's play area under 5's. Paper/milk ordering, 400m from pub.

£££

Directions: At the A14 roundabout (Junction 60), take the last exit, signposted 'Felixstowe Docks' and camping. Go straight over the next roundabout (Junction 62), signposted 'Town Centre'. Turn left after the roundabout, signposted 'Peewit Caravan Park'. The tree lined drive is easy to miss, look out for the large, but subtle sign.

GPS: N51°57.298'E001°19.603'
OS grid: 169 TM 288 337

Easter - October

ENGLAND

[19] Church Farm Holiday Park

Church Farm Road, Aldeburgh, Suffolk,
IP15 5DW Tel: 08445 580497
www.amberleisure.com

This pleasant campsite is across the road from a large stony beach. Pitches are large and hedges provide shelter and privacy. There are no sea views from the site, but nearby Aldeburg is an idyllic seaside town with nice restaurants, and an olde worlde high street. Tractors haul fishing boats up the pebble beach, and their catches are for sale from wooden huts. The editors really liked this area. There is a walking/cycling path along the sea front to Thorpeness, another pretty place with a mere and rowing boats.

| NA | 30 | NP | 62 | 16 AMP | |

Old town 5 minutes. Town centre 15 minutes.

£££

Directions: Travelling south on the A12, turn left onto the A1094, signposted 'Aldeburgh'. Follow the A1094 for five miles and at the roundabout, take the second exit, signposted 'Caravan Park'. The caravan park is signposted on the left just before the sea front. If you have not been to Aldeburgh perhaps you should, it is enchanting.

GPS: N52°09.567'E001°36.135'
OS grid: 156 TM 464 573

March - October

[20] The Vulcan Arms CL

Vulcan Arms, Sizewell, Leiston, Suffolk,
IP16 4UD Tel: 01728 830 748
www.caravanclub.co.uk

This CL is in the grounds of the Vulcan Arms pub, which offers real ale and home cooked food. There are no sea views, but it is only 100 yards walk along a footpath from the beach. There are coastal footpaths south to Thorpeness and enchanting Aldeburgh, and north to Dunwich. Sizewell is a pleasant little hamlet with a café close to the beach and small boats stored on a grassy dune.

| NA | 1/2 | NP | 5 | 16 AMP x 4 | |

Dog friendly pub. Café 2 minutes.

£££

Directions: Heading south on the B1122, 700m before Leiston, turn left, signposted 'Sizewell Beach' and 'Household Waste Centre', onto Lovers Lane. Travel towards the sea and The Vulcan Arms is opposite the entrance to Sizewell power station in 2.2 miles. From Leiston, turn right at the traffic lights opposite the White Horse Hotel to Sizewell, signposted 'Aldeburgh'. Turn left, signposted 'Sizewell' and continue until the T-junction, turning left onto Lovers Lane. Travel towards the sea and The Vulcan Arms is opposite the entrance to Sizewell power station in 2.2 miles.

GPS: N52°12.433'E001°37.185'
OS grid: 156 TM 473 627

All Year

21
Cliff House Caravan Park

Cliff House Park, Sizewell Common, Leiston, Suffolk, IP16 4TU Tel: 01728 830724
www.cliffhousepark.co.uk

This level campsite is located alongside the beach. There are 60 touring pitches but, because it is level, only the front row has a sea view over a low wall with sympathetic planting. The sea view café/bar, which is also reception, is in a white building alongside the beach. The disabled facilities and showers have just been revamped and the toilets are next. To get to the sea from the campsite, you cross the coastal path and then 50m of grassy dune that slopes down to the pebbled beach. Anglers can fish from the beach and fishing boats are launched from the beach near the Café. The Vulcan Arms pub/CL is a half mile walk north.

| NA | 12 | | NP | 60 | | 10/16 AMP | | |

| WC | | | | | | | MG | MB |

Games room, café/bar onsite.

£££ 🐕 ††† M (i) WiFi
£5 day £10 week

Directions: Heading south on the B1122, 700m before Leiston, turn left, signposted 'Sizewell Beach' and 'Household Waste Centre', onto Lovers Lane. In two miles, having travelled under the electric pylons from Sizewell, turn right, signposted 'Sizewell Hall'. The caravan park is 300m down a narrow road with passing places. Take the left fork at the country house gates, signposted 'Caravan Park', into a narrow, gated entrance on a single-track lane with passing places.

GPS: N52°12.164'E001°37.145'
OS grid: 156 TM 472 622

March - November

22
Cliff House Holiday Park

Minsmere Road, Dunwich, Suffolk, IP17 3DQ
Tel: 01728 648282
www.cliffhouseholidays.co.uk

Set in the grounds of an old country house estate, this family holiday park has 120 camping and touring pitches, available by the night, some of which have sea views. The park is adjacent to the National Trust's Dunwich Heath, woodlands and the Minsmere Bird Reserve. The site has a new bar and restaurant and has function rooms available for weddings and corporate events. There is a barbeque area, 24-hour warden, bike hire and forest glade camping by the beach. There are 63 steps down to the large and quiet gravel beach.

| NA | 33 | | NP | 104 | | 10 AMP | | |

| WC | | | | | | | MG | MB |

WiFi in bar and reception.

£££ 🐕 ††† M (i) WiFi

Directions: Travelling north on the B1125 from Westleton, take the right turn after the Westleton sign, signposted 'Dunwich'. Follow the Dunwich road for approximately two miles. Turn right, signposted 'Cliff House', then the third left, signposted 'Cliff House Inn and caravan site'.

GPS: N52°15.693'E001°37.606'
OS grid: 156 TM 475 688

March - October

23
Southwold Harbour

Ferry Road, Southwold, Suffolk, IP18 6ND
Tel: 01502 722486 www.waveney.gov.uk/Leisure/
Caravan+and+Camping/southwold_campsite.htm

This site has a festival feel to it; it is flat, open, and is popular with families and groups in tents. Unfortunately, the site had not been keeping on top of cleaning its facilities when we inspected. This site has water on two sides where a river meets the sea, but has views of neither. The beach is only 100m from the site, and a 10 minute (one mile) walk along a footpath will take you to Southwold and its beach huts. Southwold is also the home to the Adnams brewery.

NA 5	NP 162	0 AMP

Shop opposite.

£££

Directions: Take the A1035 to Southwold. Follow the road through High Street then round to the right into Queens Street, then left at the T-junction onto Ferry Road. Follow Ferry Road past the seafront and the site is on your right just before a 90-degree right hand bend.

GPS: N52°18.938'E001°40.368'
OS grid: 156 TM 504 749

April - October

24
Heathland Beach Caravan Park

London Road, Kessingland, Nr Lowestoft,
Suffolk, NR33 7PJ Tel: 01502 740337
www.heathlandbeach.co.uk

This family friendly holiday park has static caravans overlooking the sea and, should you get up early enough, you can walk down to the large sand beach and watch the sunrise. The site has private fishing lakes, all weather tennis courts, and three heated swimming pools, one with a small water slide. Hard surfaced roads run around the touring meadow with statics on three sides. Hedgerows between the pitches provide privacy and pathways are low-lit. The large, sandy, quiet beach is accessed along a 200m footpath, followed by 97 steps.

NA 25	NP 64	15 AMP	MG	MB

Village shops 10 mins. WiFi free in bar.

£££   WiFi
                                    Free in bar

Directions: Travelling south away from Lowestoft on the A12, drive into the countryside and take the first exit at the roundabout onto the B1437 (this is straight on). Take the next left, signed 'Heathland Caravan Site'. The site is on the left in one mile.

GPS: N52°25.724'E001°43.309'
OS grid: 156 TM 532 877

April/Easter - November

ENGLAND

Kessingland Beach Holiday Park [25]

Beach Road, Kessingland, Nr Lowestoft, Suffolk, NR33 7RW
Tel: 08440 502563 www.park-resorts.com/
holiday-parks/east-anglia/kessingland-beach/

This site is right on the beachfront and has direct beach access. 24 of the statics for hire have uninterrupted sea views, but unfortunately, this site places its emphasis on statics and the touring pitches are farthest from the sea in a hollow. There are lots of facilities including: fish and chips, a mini market, entertainment, and arcades. The shingle beach adjacent to the site goes on for miles, stretching all the way up to Lowestoft and down to Southwold, providing plenty of room for walking, bathing or simply relaxing.

| NA | 5 | | NP | 100+ | 16 AMP | | |

£££

Directions: Travelling towards Lowestoft on the A12, take the right turn at the roundabout onto the B1437, signposted 'Kessingland Beach'. Follow the road to the seafront, round to the right, then straight on. The site is at end of the road.

GPS: N52°24.467'E001°43.609'
OS grid: 156 TM 535 854

Easter - October

White House Beach Caravan Club Site [26]

Beach Road, Kessingland, Lowestoft, Suffolk, NR33 7RW Tel: 01502 740278
www.caravanclub.co.uk

This site offers the best sea view pitches for miles in either direction. You can watch the huge ships on the horizon as you gaze over a large gravel wilderness littered with wild flowers. The beach road splits the site in two; 22 pitches are beachside, and trees and shrubs enclose the majority on the other side of the road. The Lowestoft – Southwold bus stop is a half mile walk. Kessingland beach is shingle but becomes sandy towards Lowestoft. The beach is quiet and dog friendly all year.

| NA | 7.5 | | NP | 115 | 16 AMP | | |

Restaurant 300 yards.

£££

Directions: Travelling towards Lowestoft on the A12, take the right turn at the roundabout onto the B1437, signposted 'Kessingland Beach'. Follow the road to the seafront and round to the right. The site is both sides of the road.

GPS: N52°24.665'E001°43.618'
OS grid: 156 TM 535 857

March - October

Pakefield Caravan Park [27]

Arbor Lane, Pakefield, Lowestoft, Suffolk,
NR33 7BE Tel: 01502 561136
www.pakefieldpark.co.uk

Static caravans occupy most of this site. There are 12 touring pitches tucked away on their own pleasant area at the back of the site, but have no sea views. Tourers have full use of the facilities, including an outdoor pool, children's playground, and the clubhouse with resident entertainer. The pin coded toilet block is modern and all facilities have full mobility access. The wide shingle beach is only a short walk from the touring field.

| NA | 15 | NP | 12 | 16 AMP | | |

WC | | | | | | |

£££   Several hot spots

Directions: Travelling towards Lowestoft from Kessingland, turn right at the third roundabout, signposted 'Beach Farm' then follow signposts to 'Pakefield Caravan Park' through residential streets. The site is on the right hand side of a left hand bend.

enjoyEngland.com
★★★★
HOLIDAY PARK

GPS: N52°26.866'E001°43.791'
OS grid: 156-134 TM 535 898

March - October

Great Yarmouth Racecourse Caravan Club Site [28]

Jellicoe Road, Great Yarmouth, Norfolk,
NR30 4AU Tel: 01493 855223
www.caravanclub.co.uk

Located inside the racetrack at Yarmouth Racecourse, this site has all grass pitches. The beach is only 400m away over a raised road with pavements. Also close by is an 18 hole golf course. There are good public transport links to Great Yarmouth with its six acre pleasure beach and plenty of traditional seaside attractions.

| NA | 4 | NP | 115 | 16 AMP | | |

WC | | | | | MG | MB |

£££

Directions: From Great Yarmouth, follow the A149 and signposts to Caister. Turn off the A149, signposted 'Racecourse' and 'Camping'. The site entrance is on the left past the racecourse entrance. Non-members welcome.

enjoyEngland.com
★★★★★
TOURING & CAMPING PARK

GPS: N52°37.726'E001°44.057'
OS grid: 134 TG 527 099

March - October

ENGLAND

Long Beach Estate Caravan Park/ 29 Hemsby Tent and Touring Site

Long Beach Estate Company, Estate Office,
Long Beach, Hemsby, Great Yarmouth, NR29 4JD
Tel: 01493 730023 www.long-beach.co.uk

This is a quirky site with two distinctly different camping areas. The main camping area is 500m inland, on two flat fields with a modern toilet block. The quirky camping is amongst sea view houses owned by Long Beach and available for rent. From here you look over the two massive sand dunes with a valley separating them, known as Great Winterton Valley, a 40 acre Site of Special Scientific Interest. Both the Long Beach site and the Hemsby touring site, which is 5 minute walk from Long Beach, have full access to the facilities at Long Beach and the WiFi access has been extended to cover Hemsby.

NA	15	NP	175	10-16 AMP		
WC	🚿			0	MG	MB

Dishwashing facilities at Long Beach. Toilet waste disposal at Long Beach - lift manhole. Bar onsite.

£££ 🐕 ♛ M ⓘ WiFi

£3, £15 per week

Directions: Travelling south on the B1159 from Winterton on Sea to Hemsby, at the roundabout in Hemsby, take the left-hand turn, signposted 'Long Beach'. Take the second left into Kings Loke, signposted 'Camping'. The park is at the end of the road. Do not use the postcode in your Sat-nav it will take you the wrong way.

GPS: N52°42.002'E001°41.845'
OS grid: 134 TG 502 177

March - November

Waxham Sands Holiday Park 30

Warren Farm, Horsey, Nr. Great Yarmouth,
Norfolk, NR29 4EJ Tel: 01692 598325
www.waxhamsandsholidaypark.co.uk

21-26ft max.

This family friendly campsite has been run by the same owner for the past 16 years. There is no sea view, but the site is protected by a large sand dune and has a half mile stretch of private beach, which is as good as it gets. Seals can be seen both in the sea and on the beach. This site has four toilet blocks, as well as ample disabled facilities, and fully tiled shower blocks for men and women. It is, and deserves to be, a busy campsite, so if it's full, try the nearby Walnut Farm CS.

NA	12	NP	200	16 AMP		
WC	🚿			0	MG	MB

Showers 50p token.

££ 🐕 ♛ M ⓘ WiFi

Directions: The campsite is located between Horsey and Waxham on the B1159 and is well signposted on the road. Drive down the long drive, with passing places, to the site. GPS co-ordinates were taken at the top of the drive.

GPS: N52°45.462'E001°38.135'
OS grid: 134 TTG 459 245

May - September

31
The Manor Caravan Park

Happisburgh, Norwich, Norfolk, NR12 0PW
Tel: 01692 652228

There are excellent sea views from every pitch on this site as the campground slopes gently down towards the unfenced cliff. The beach is accessible from the site via 53 metal steps. The beach is dog friendly and still has some WW2 beach defences. The coastal path stretches up to Walcott along unfenced cliffs with spectacular views. The site is also adjacent to the village, with a proper country pub just outside the campsite entrance. The editors really liked this simple site.

| NA | 10 | NP | 40 | 6 with electric |

Directions: Take the B1159 towards Happisburg. In Happisburg the turning is easy to miss, it is on the left after the bend by the church. Drive to the right of the pub, down a narrow gravel track.

GPS: N52°49.489'E001°31.902'
OS grid: 133 TG 380 311

April - October

32
Sandy Gulls Caravan Park

Cromer Road, Mundesley, Norfolk, NR11 8DF   Tel: 01263 720 513

For 27 years this quiet, traditional site has been beautifully chaired for by the same family. The terraced pitches provide expansive sea views. The cliff prevents direct beach acces but it only takes two minutes to walk down to the beach and 10 minutes back up. The wide, sandy beach still has some of the WW2 defences and stretches for miles down past Mundesly with its Blue Flag award winning beach, colourful beach huts and attractive family resort village.

| NA | 10 | NP | 30-46 | 6/5 AMP |

Pub 500 metres. Laundry handwashing only.

Directions: Exit Mundesley on the coast road (B1159) towards Cromer. The site is on the right hand side, signposted.

GPS: N52°53.195'E001°25.060'
OS grid: 133 TG 302 373

March - December

Seacroft Caravan Club Site `33`

Runton Road, Cromer, Norfolk, NR27 9NH
Tel: 01263 514938
www.caravanclub.co.uk

This site has more character than most Caravan Club sites as it has a bar, restaurant, and a small outdoor pool, and is, of course, up to the usual high standards. Although the sea can be seen from site, the walk to the beach is a long one. The surrounding area boasts a charming golf course, plus sea and freshwater fishing. There is a bus stop just outside the site for transport to the area's many attractions.

| NA | 7.5 | | NP | 130 | | 16 AMP | | |

£££

WiFi £5hr, non members welcome

Directions: Exit Cromer towards Sheringham along the A149 and the site is on the left-hand side.

GPS: N52°56.037'E001°16.758'
OS grid: 133 TG 205 424

April - January

Woodhill Park `34`

Cromer Road, East Runton, Norfolk,
NR27 9PX Tel: 01263 512 242
www.woodhill-park.com

This site is located on a cliff top between Cromer and Sheringham at East Runton. There are views of the sea from the top right end of the site and the touring pitches have good views of the coastline and surrounding countryside. The site is popular, but still tranquil. There is a good children's play area with a sandpit, swings and assault course and the recreation field has a petanque court, tennis nets, football goalposts and crazy golf. Large vehicles must book in advance.

| NA | 39 | | NP | 300 | | 16 AMP | | |

Beach 10 minutes.

£££

Directions: Take the A148 into Cromer. Drive past Halfords and Carpet Right and turn left at the roundabout signposted Sheringham (A149). Drive to the end of Beach road and turn left, at the T-junction, along the seafront. Drive 1.4 miles passing through East Runton and the site entrance is on your right with a bus stop opposite.

GPS: N52°56.222'E001°15.739'
OS grid: 133 TG 194 427

All Year

35
Laburnum Caravan Park

Water Lane, West Runton, Norfolk,
NR27 9QP Tel: 01263 837473
www.laburnumcaravanpark.co.uk

This family run park has 170 mostly privately owned static caravans, and just six touring pitches but all with panoramic sea views. There is a secure children's playground with swings, slide, etc, a large recreation field, football pitch and hard tennis court all set away from the caravans. Because the site is on top of a cliff, there is a five minute walk to the beach. West Runton is a short walk away and has local shops, a Village Inn and an animal sanctuary. The campsite does not take card payments.

| NA | 13 | NP | 6 | 16 AMP | | |

| WC | | | | | MG | MB |

Beach 5 minutes, social club 3 minutes.

£££

Directions: Take the A148 into Cromer. Shortly after you pass the White Horse Inn on your left, at the junction, take the left hand fork onto the A149. Follow this road until West Runton. In West Runton, take the right turn shortly after the petrol station, by the Village Inn, signposted 'P', 'Beach' and 'Caravan'. The entrance to the site is on the left fork at the end of the road, well signposted.

GPS: N52°56.407'E001°14.682'
OS grid: 133 TG 181 429

Easter - October

36
Beeston Regis
Caravan and Camping Park

Cromer Road, West Runton, Cromer,
Norfolk NR27 9QZ Tel: 01263 823614
www.beestonregis.co.uk

Much of this site is occupied by privately owned statics, but there is a separate field, adjacent to the pebble church, which has 41 touring pitches. All the pitches are large, clearly marked and have sea views; it is possible to book one for the entire season. The touring field has its own toilet block and a laundry with a library (a novel idea). There are two camping fields available for groups or rallies. There is a long coastal footpath with steps down to the large beach.

| NA | 60 | NP | 41 | 16 AMP | | |

| WC | | | | | MG | MB |

£££

Directions: Adjacent to the A149 between West Runton and Sheringham. The site is on the left when travelling from Sheringham, opposite Beeston Hall, and is well signposted. Follow the instructions on the board after the left turn.

enjoyEngland.com
★★★★
HOLIDAY, TOURING & CAMPING PARK

GPS: N52°56.374'E001°13.992'
OS grid: 133 TG 173 430

Easter - October

ENGLAND

High Sand Creek Campsite [37]

The Greenway, Stiffkey,
Norfolk, NR23 1QF
Tel: 01328 830235

This is a family campsite overlooking an amazing salt marsh, where you can you can swim in the creeks and waterholes as long as you keep a close eye on the tide. There is a sandy beach beyond and it is approximately 20 minutes walk to the sea. This is a site for a Swallows and Amazons style holiday where you make your own entertainment. Wildlife watching is popular as there are seals on the sandbanks at Blakeney Point and a wide variety of interesting birds. There is a freezer available for freezer blocks. The editors really liked this site and surroundings.

| NA | 6 | NP | 80 | 0 AMP | | |

| WC | | | | | | MG | MB |

Shop 5 minutes walk.

£££ 🐕 ⅈⅈ M ⅈ WiFi

Directions: Travelling towards Kings Lynn on the A149, travel through Stiffkey village (tight with passing places), and turn right, signed 'Camping'. Listed C+CC and signposted 'Greenway unadopted' next to a red post box.

GPS: N52°57.136'E000°55.480'
OS grid: 132 TF 964 437

March - October

Pinewoods Holiday Park [38]

Beach Road, Wells-Next-the-Sea, Norfolk,
NR23 1DR Tel: 01328 710439
www.pinewoods.co.uk

This site is all about the beach and quirky town. There are no sea views from the site, but the sandy beach, with its quirky beach huts available for hire, is only four minutes walk away. The shallow water is particularly child friendly, and adults will be kept amused with the comings and goings of boats from the harbour. You can walk along the sea defence to town, which is just big enough to cater for most tourist needs. The local Nature Reserve and salt marshes are good for bird watching.

| NA | 10 | NP | 155 | 16 AMP | | |

| WC | | | | | | MG | MB |

Pub 5-7 minutes walk.

£££ 🐕 ⅈⅈ M ⅈ WiFi

Directions: From Sherringham, follow the A149 into Wells-Next-the-Sea. Once in town, follow signs to the beach on the B1105 down to the harbour. At the harbour, take the left turn, signposted 'Pinewoods Camping'. The campsite is on the left before the beach parking.

GPS: N52°58.164'E000°50.962'
OS grid: 132 TF 914 450

March - October

Manor Park Holiday Village [39]

Manor Park, Hunstanton, Norfolk,
PE36 5AZ Tel: 01485 532300
www.manor-park.co.uk

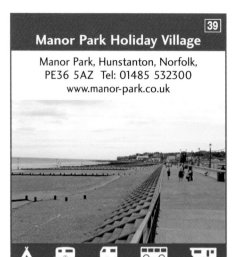

1200 Statics

This is a large, lodge park with a small touring area near the entrance. There are no sea views, but Hunstanton's wide, sandy, family friendly beach is two minutes walk away. The walk to town along the promenade takes five minutes. Onsite there are two outdoor, heated swimming pools, an arcade, children's club, and a bar/restaurant with evening entertainments. Season pitches are available and static, privately owned caravans and lodges have 11-month occupancy; this would be a good place for full timers to buy a property.

NA 35   NP 65   16 AMP

Swimming pool opposite Tescos.

£££   WiFi

£15 per week

Directions: From the King's Lynn bypass take the A149 to Hunstanton. As you enter Hunstanton, at the first roundabout take the second exit onto the B1161, signposted 'Seafront' and 'South Beach'. At the second roundabout turn left and Manor Park is on your left.

GPS: N52°55.865'E000°29.162'
OS grid: 132 TF 671 399

April - October

North Shore Holiday Centre Complex [40]

Elmhirst Avenue, Roman Bank, Skegness, Lincolnshire,
PE25 1SL Tel: 01754 763815 / 762051
www.northshore-skegness.co.uk/tourers.php

There are no sea views from this family friendly holiday park, but it is the nearest site to Skegness. There is a large touring field accessed by hard roads, and the pitches are gravelled for all year use. The campsite has a pitch and putt and crazy golf course, and opposite there is an 18 hole golf course with practice area and putting green. The large, sandy beach is a five minute walk away alongside the golf course. The beach in front of the golf course is quiet and you can walk along the beach for 20 minutes to Skegness.

NA 40   NP 133   10 & 6 AMP

Beach 5 minutes. Slipway 3 miles at Jackson's Corner.

£££   WiFi

Directions: From the centre of Skegness, take the A52, signposted 'North Shore'. The site is adjacent to the main road on the left hand side, clearly signposted.

GPS: N53°09.294'E000°20.550'
OS grid: 122 TF 566 645

March - November

ENGLAND

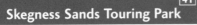

Skegness Sands Touring Park `41`

Winthorpe Avenue, Skegness, Lincolnshire,
PE25 1QZ Tel: 01754 761484
www.skegness-sands.com

This is a privately owned, caravan club affiliated touring site. The site has private access to the promenade and is adjacent to the large sandy beach, but only a small number of grass pitches benefit from a sea view. The rest of the pitches are a mix of grass and hard standing. As part of a larger complex, the site has a good number of facilities including a heated swimming pool, children's play area, and a hairdressing salon. There is a bus stop adjacent to the site and Skegness is only two miles away. Large motorhomes and 5th wheels must book in advance.

| NA | 5 | NP | 82 | 16 AMP | | |

Grey water disposal; manhole. Swimming pool May - September. Arcade and bar bottom of road - 1 minute.

£££

Member £20.80 non £27.80

Directions: From the centre of Skegness, take the A52, signposted 'Mablethorpe' and 'Ingoldmells'. After approximately one metre, turn right opposite the Garden City Pub into Winthorpe Avenue. The site is on the left in 200yds.

GPS: N53°10.214'E000°20.918'
OS grid: 122 TF 571 658

All Year

Skegness Water Leisure Park `42`

Walls Lane, Ingoldmells, Skegness,
Lincolnshire, PE25 1JF Tel: 01754 899400
www.skegnesswaterleisurepark.co.uk

This unique holiday park is set in 185 acres of landscaped countryside without a sea view, but just five minute walk from the large sandy beaches of Skegness and Butlins. There are a wide variety of facilities onsite, including the Barn Inn, children's play area, licensed coffee shop, Lincolnshire Coast Light Railway, cable tow water-skiing, and five acre course fishing lake and tackle shop. Some pitches are lakeside, so you can watch either tranquil fishing or cable skiing. This site is very pleasant and equally suits adults and children.

| NA | 188 | NP | 500 | 16 AMP | | |

Café. Waterskiing lake.

£££

Directions: From the centre of Skegness, take the A52, signposted 'Mablethorpe' and 'Ingoldmells'. Turn left just before the traffic lights, signposted 'Water Leisure Park'. Follow the road, turning left onto the park when signed.

GPS: N53°10.602'E000°20.533'
OS grid: 122 TF 566 669

March - October

43 Butlins Leisure

Skegness Resort, Lincolnshire, PE25 1NJ
Tel: 01754 762 311
www.butlins.com/resorts/skegness

Butlins Skegness is located right next to a long stretch of sandy beach with direct access to the promenade that stretches all the way to Ingoldmells. The campsite is inland, on the other side of a busy road. We were unable to inspect the campground, but it is safe to assume that all the necessary facilities are available. All the usual activities you might expect from a Butlins resort are available including a new spa exclusive to Skegness. There are bus stops on both sides of the road, just outside the site entrance.

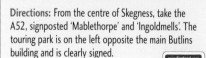

| NA | 30 | NP | 174 | 16 AMP |

Lift manhole.

££££ 🐕 †† M ⓘ WiFi

Directions: From the centre of Skegness, take the A52, signposted 'Mablethorpe' and 'Ingoldmells'. The touring park is on the left opposite the main Butlins building and is clearly signed.

GPS: N53°10.953'E000°20.909'
OS grid: 122 TF 570 676

Easter - October

44 Hardy's Touring Park

Sea Lane, Ingoldmells, Skegness,
Lincolnshire PE25 1PG
Tel: 01754 874071

700m from Ingoldmells' large, sandy beach, and right in the thick of things, you will love or loath this location, but it is definitely not the spot for a quiet weekend. Fantasy Island theme park is adjacent and you can watch people on the rollercoaster. You can also play bingo for free from your pitch, as you'll hear the bingo caller across the site. There is a large pub and a McDonalds nearby. The pitches are close together, but as this is the only touring park in static caravan land, it is an oasis and deserves the title of Cool Camping. Large vehicles must book in advance.

| NA | 8 | NP | 130 | 10 AMP |

Beach 800yards.

£££ 🐕 †† M ⓘ WiFi

Directions: Travelling on the A52 from Skegness, when you reach Ingoldmells take the right turn next to the Ship Inn onto Sea Lane. The site is on the right hand side, signposted, next to Fantasy Island.

GPS: N53°11.574'E000°20.588'
OS grid: 122 TF 561 688

March - October

ENGLAND

County Meadows `45`

Anchor Lane, Ingoldmells, Skegness, Lincolnshire PE25 1LZ Tel: 01754 874455
www.countrymeadows.co.uk

This is a family run site located five minutes (700m) from the beach and a short way from the kiss me quick entertainments of Ingoldmells. This is a midsized, flat campsite with a small fishing lake at the far end and a children's play area. The grass is well kept and this site has a clam, peaceful atmosphere. Large vehicles (maximum 20ft) must book in advance.

| NA 7 | NP 220 | 10 AMP | | |
| WC | | | | MG | MB |

Token for shower 30p. Slipway Jackson's Corner 5 minutes drive. Beach 700m.

£££

Directions: Follow the A52 from Skegness through Ingoldmells towards Chapel St Leonards. Turn right at the traffic lights, signposted 'Fantasy Island' 'P'. Follow the road for approximately 1km and the site is on the left.

GPS: N53°12.014'E000°20.430'
OS grid: 122 TF 564 695

Easter - October

Eastfields Park `46`

Chapel Point, Chapel St Leonards, Skegness, Lincolnshire, PE24 5UX Tel: 01754 874499
www.eastfieldspark.co.uk

There are no sea views from this established touring park comprising of 60 hard standing pitches for touring caravans and motorhomes, all with electric hook-up points and adjacent car parking. There is a well-stocked fishing lake onsite. The site is on the outskirts of Chapel St Leonards and is the closest in the area to the sea, being just across the road from a very large sandy beach with a beach café and parking (at £1 per day). The nearest pub is only four minutes walk and serves local beer and restaurant food.

| NA 4 | NP 60 | 10 AMP | | |
| WC | | | | MG | MB |

Pub 4 minutes. Shop opposite. Slipway 400m.

£££

Directions: Travelling on the A52 from Ingoldmells, take the left turn after Chapel Garden Centre, signposted 'Chapel St Leonards'. Travel to the end of the road and at the junction turn left, and then sharp right onto St Leonards Drive. Follow this road out of Chapel St Leonards to Chapel Point. The site is on the left, signposted.

GPS: N53°13.990'E000°20.214'
OS grid: 122 TF 559 733

April - October

Wyndhaven CL [47]

Anderby Road, Chapel St Leonards,
Lincolnshire, Skegness, PE24 5XQ
Tel: 01754 872486

This is a pretty orchard site adjacent to the coast road, just past Chapel Point. This has all the charm of a rural CL, but with the convenience of the sea and beach just across the road. There is no sea view as the site is lower than the road.

NA 1   NP 5   0 AMP

Pub 1/2 mile. Slipway 2 minutes.

£££

Directions: Travelling on the A52 from Ingoldmells, take the left turn towards Chapel St Leonards after Chapel Garden Centre, signposted 'Chapel St Leonards'. Travel to the end of the road and at the junction turn left, and then sharp right onto St Leonards Drive. Follow this road out of Chapel St Leonards to Chapel Point. The site entrance is on the left, clearly signposted.

GPS: N53°14.272'E000°20.179'
OS grid: 122 TF 559 737

March - October

Seacroft [48]

Sutton Road, Trusthorpe, Mablethorpe,
Lincolnshire, LN12 2PN Tel: 01507 472421
http://seacroftholidays.co.uk

This family owned park has direct access to the beach, but there are no sea views. Predominantly lodges and chalets occupy the site, but there are spacious pitches for tourers. The onsite clubhouse boasts 'Tastes of Lincolnshire' locally sourced produce, on the menu. The park has its own private fishing lake. A one mile walk along the promenade with pleasant sea views takes you to the town of Mablethorpe.

NA 18   NP 13   16 AMP

Slipway at Sandylands.

£££   WiFi Free

Directions: On the A52 between Sutton on Sea and Mablethorpe. The park is on the right when travelling towards Mablethorpe, signposted.

GPS: N53°19.552'E000°16.344'
OS grid: 122 TF 514 833

March - October

ENGLAND

49
Golden Sands

Quebec Road, Mablethorpe, Lincolnshire,
LN12 1QJ Tel: 0871 2310884
www.haven.com/parks/yorkshire_lincolnshire/golden_sands/index.aspx

This is an ideal site for a family holiday, with lots of activities for adults and kids alike. There are indoor and outdoor pools, both with flumes, as well as go-karts, mini ten-pin bowling, coarse fishing, fencing and archery. The large touring site is separated from the static area and is furthest from the sea, which is across the road and over the dunes. Autumn and winter provide the opportunity to combine a bracing walk on the beach with the chance to see grey seals as this area is one of the UK's largest breeding grounds.

| NA | 20 | NP | 224 | 16 AMP | | |

| WC | | | | | |

£££

Directions: Follow the A52 through Mablethorpe. Just after the Louth Hotel Pub on your left, take the right turn, signposted 'Seafront'. Travel to the end of the road and turn left, signposted 'P' and 'Seal Sanctuary'. The site is on the left in approximately one mile, well signposted.

GPS: N53°21.207'E000°15.129'
OS grid: 122 TF 496 866

March - October

50
Seaside Caravan Park

Sand Lane, Ulrome, Driffield, North
Humberside, YO25 8TT Tel: 01262 468228
www.seaside-caravan-park.co.uk

This is a quiet and comfortable site located on a small cliff, adjacent to a safe, sandy beach. Pitches are large and well spaced, and the toilet block is adequate and clean. This is the sort of area where little changes from year to year, apart from natural coastal erosion. There is a fish and chip shop within walking distance.

| NA | 10 | NP | 140 | 10 AMP | | |

| WC | | | | | |

Pub walking distance.

£££

Directions: Travel six miles south of Bridlington on the A165 and turn left onto the B1242 (Allison Lane) to Ulrome. In 1.3 miles, when you see the village sign/flower planter, turn left at the grass triangle and proceed onto Main Street/Sand Lane towards the sea. The campsite entrance is on the left in 270m.

GPS: N53°59.727'W000°12.742'
OS grid: 107 TA 173 574

March - October

Filey Brigg 51
Caravan and Country Park

Church Cliff Drive, North Cliff,
Filey, North Yorkshire, YO14 9ET
Tel: 01723 513852

This Local Authority owned site overlooks the sea. The modern, clean, and well-kept toilet block has a card entry system. Onsite there is a well-stocked shop and a nice café that has a good vegetarian option. The beach is a short downhill walk away, and you can walk a little further to Filey where there are plenty of restaurants, bars and shops.

| NA 9 | NP 158 | 0 AMP | |
| WC | | | |

Shop onsite.

£££

Directions: Follow signs from the A165 through Filey to the country park.

GPS: N54°12.865'W000°17.272'
OS grid: 101 TA 118 813

April - October

Whitby Holiday Park 52

Salt Wick Bay, Whitby, North Yorkshire,
YO22 4JX Tel: 01947 602664
www.whitbypark.co.uk

Overlooking the sweep of Saltwick Bay, this park commands spectacular views of the coastline in a beautifully rural, cliff top setting. This is a large, tidy, commercial site with many static caravans, but most of the cliff top area is given over to tourers. There is a steep sandy cliff path to the isolated sand and rock pool beach. There are excellent facilities for all the family. This is a great campsite.

| NA 4 | NP 120 | 16 AMP | |
| WC | | | MG | MB |

Pub, shop and slipway at Whitby.

£££

Directions: From Scarborough take the A171 through Hawkser, turn right following signs to the Y.H.A. The site is on the right two miles down the lane. Final approach road very narrow.

GPS: N54°28.778'W000°35.510'
OS grid: 94 NZ 916 108

March - October

Sandfield House Farm Caravan Park

53

Sandsend Road, Whitby, North Yorkshire, YO21 3SR Tel: 01947 602660
www.sandfieldhousefarm.co.uk

This is one of the few sea view sites that can boast the accolade of being awarded 5 Stars. The grounds are impeccable and there is an attractive, stone built, modern, central heated amenities block. The park is set in undulating countryside and care has been taken to ensure that all pitches are level. From many of the pitches there are glorious sea views. The beach is within reasonable walking distance and there are walks with glorious scenery and panoramic views of the sea.

NA 12 NP 70 10 AMP

WC MG MB

Pub 15 minutes.

£££ M WiFi

Directions: From Whitby, travel one mile north on the A174. The site is on the main road on your left, opposite Whitby Golf Course.

enjoyEngland.com ★★★★★ TOURING PARK

GPS: N54°29.507'W000°38.568'
OS grid: 94 NZ 878 114

March - October

Hooks House Farm

54

Raw Pasture Bank, Robin Hoods Bay, Whitby, Yorkshire, YO22 4PE Tel: 01947 880283
www.hookshousefarm.co.uk

© Jill Halder

Situated on a working farm, this family run campsite provides a relaxed and pleasant atmosphere for all campers. Panoramic sea views of Robin Hoods Bay and countryside views are clearly visible from every pitch. Although shops and pubs are within easy walking distance, the sea is 20 minutes walk downhill. The campsite's owners also offer livery for people wishing to bring their horses.

NA 5 NP 25 10 AMP

WC MG MB

Pub, shop and slipway 1/2 mile at Robin Hoods Bay.

£££ M WiFi

Directions: Travel three miles south from Whitby on the A171 and turn left at Hawsker, signposted 'Robin Hoods Bay' on the B1447. The site is clearly visible on the right in two miles.

GPS: N54°26.325'W000°32.575'
OS grid: 94 NZ 945 058

All Year

55
Crimdon House Farm CS

Coast Road, Hartlepool, County Durham,
TS27 3AA Tel: 01429 272526
www.siteseeker.co.uk

This is a classic CS. The site has an elevated position and occupies a fairly level, three quarters of an acre, well mown field close to a farm. There are beautiful wide views across a large field, over the dunes to the sea, which is only a quarter of a mile away and accessible down a National Cycle Way. The site is also at the start of an 11 mile coastal footpath north to Seaham harbour.

| NA | 1 | | NP | 5 | | 0 AMP | | |
| WC | | | | | | MG | | MB |

Pub and shop 1 mile.

£££ 🐕 ‖‖ M ⓘ WiFi

Directions: From the A19 take the A179 to Hartlepool. At the third roundabout take the A1086 north for Blackhall/Horden. The site is on the right immediately past the green bridge, turn down a farm lane that is easy to miss.

GPS: N54°43.287'W001°15.412'
OS grid: 93 NZ 483 365

All Year

56
Sandhaven Caravan Site

Bents Park Road, South Shields, Tyne and
Wear, NE33 2NL Tel: 01670 860256
www.northumbrianleisure.co.uk/SandHaven.html

This park is in the heart of the action, adjacent to South Shields golden, sandy beach. Static, privately owned caravans occupy most of this high quality site. The site has relocated their touring pitches around the park, at the time of publishing 20-25 new hard standing touring pitches were under construction and some will have a view of the sea. A new toilet block was also under construction. The beach is perfect for sandcastle building and you can watch the boats coming and going from the Tyne. You are spoilt for choice when choosing a meal in this cosmopolitan area.

| NA | 3 | | NP | 25 | | 16 AMP | | |
| WC | | | | | | MG | | MB |

Pub, shop and slipway 5 minutes.

£££ 🐕 ‖‖ M ⓘ WiFi

Directions: From the A19 turn onto the A185. Follow signs for the seafront/South Shields Beach until you reach Beach Road. Turn right onto Bents Park Road. The site is just off the beach.

GPS: N54°59.838'W001°25.033'
OS grid: 88 NZ 376 670

March - October

ENGLAND

Old Hartley Caravan Club Site 57

Whitley Bay, Tyne and Wear, NE26 4RL
Tel: 01912 370256
www.caravanclub.co.uk

Max 28ft

This slightly sloping site is perched on a grassy cliff top. The site overlooks the lighthouse on St Mary's Island, which is a local nature reserve with a bird population of national importance. The views are captivating day and night and, if that was not enough, the site is beautifully maintained with excellent facilities. Access to the sea is about five minutes walk and Whitley Bay is about 40 minutes walk.

| NA 3¹/₂ | NP 64 | 16 AMP | |

| WC | | | | MG | |

Pub 500m. Shop 1 mile.

£££   M   WiFi

Directions: Turn off the A19 three miles north of the Tyne Tunnel, at its junction with the A191, signed 'Gosforth/Whitley Bay'. Follow tourist signs for St Mary's Island. At the fourth roundabout turn left onto the A1148, signed 'Sea Front'. At the T-junction with the A193 at Whitley Bay seafront turn left signed 'Blyth'. Pass Whitley Bay Holiday Park. In two miles, at the Delaval Arms pub roundabout, turn right onto a cycle path. Fork left in 50 yards into the site entrance. Maximum 7.5m (28ft) due to access.

GPS: N55°04.533'W001°27.942'
OS grid: 88 NZ 344 748

Easter - October

Beadnell Bay Camping and Caravan Club Site 58

Beadnell, Chathill, Northumberland, NE67 5BX Tel: 01665 720586
www.siteseeker.co.uk

This large and level site is just across the main road from the sea. From site you look straight out to sea, but views are only partial because of the dunes. This site does not accommodate touring caravans nor have electric hook-ups.

An alternative site on the other side of Seahouses is about a mile away. It is right amongst the Beadnell Bay sand dunes, just 20 metres from the sea. See www.beadnellbaycaravanpark.co.uk
Tel: 01665 720589

| NA 7 | NP 150 | 0 AMP | |

| WC | | | | MG | |

Pub 5 minute walk. Shop 200 yards.

£££   M   WiFi

Directions: From the southbound A1 take the B1340, signed 'Seahouses'. At Beadnell ignore the village signs, the site is on the left just after left-hand bend.

GPS: N55°33.675'W001°38.128'
OS grid: 75 NU 231 297

May - September

Seaview Caravan Club Site `[59]`

Billendean Road, Spittal,
Berwick-upon-Tweed TD15 1QU
Tel: 01289 305198 www.caravanclub.co.uk

© Verna Stansfield

This is a long, narrow, terraced site located in an elevated position a short way back from the sea. All the pitches have either an estuary or sea view over the roof tops. The site is part sloping, but there are level pitches suitable for motorhomes. The beach is a 400m walk away.

| NA | 6 | NP | 98 | 16 AMP | | |
| WC | | | | | MG | MB |

£££ 🐕 ♀♂ M ⓘ WiFi

Directions: From the A1 north or south, take the A1167 to Tweedmouth. At the Homebase/The Bonarsteads pub roundabout take the exit east toward the sea on Billendean Terrace/Road and follow for 800m to the site.

GPS: N55°45.537'W001°59.927'
OS grid: 75 NU 003 517

Easter - December

Tarnside Caravan Park `[61]`

Tarnside, Braystones, Beckermet,
Cumbria, CA21 2YL Tel: 01946 841308
www.seacote.com

A tidy, quiet, well mown site that has been made to look attractive with tubs of flowers and a small garden. There are sea views and mountains in the far distance, but the sea views are only partial from the touring pitch area. The sandy beach is the other side of the train track, conveniently there is a Train Halt adjacent where one can catch trains to St Bees.

| NA | 3 | NP | 12 | 16 AMP | | |
| WC | | | | | MG | MB |

Pub and shop 1 mile. Slipway 4 miles at St Bees.

£££ 🐕 ♀♂ M ⓘ WiFi

Directions: Travel two miles south of Egremont on the A595 and turn right onto the B5345 (Morass Road) to Beckermet. In Beckermet centre, turn right opposite the church onto Braystones Road and travel 1.2 miles to the campsite on the left.

GPS: N54°26.537'W003°32.165'
OS grid: 89 NY 005 062

March - October

ENGLAND

Southsea Holiday and Leisure Park `4`
Melville Road, Southsea, PO4 9TB
Tel: 02392 735070
www.southsealeisurepark.com
N50°47.200'W001°02.581'
This campsite is beside the sea but has no sea view because of a grassy bank.
It is located at the very eastern end of Southsea seafront, behind Eastney swimming baths. Follow the brown tourist signs to Southsea seafront, then follow the beach road eastwards and Melville Road is the first turning on the right as you leave the seafront.

Bay View Caravan and Camping Park `5`
Old Martello Road, Pevensey Bay, East Sussex, BN24 6DX
Tel: 01323 768688
www.bay-view.co.uk
Situated next to the beach off the A259 between Pevensey Bay and Eastbourne.

Shear Barn Holiday Park `6`
Barley Lane, Hastings, Sussex. TN35 5DX
Tel: 01424 716474
www.shearbarn.co.uk
Leave the M25 at Junction 5 and follow the A21 all the way to Hastings. Follow the signs to the seafront and turn left. Follow the road round to the Stables Theatre and turn right onto Harold Road. Turn right into Gurth Road, carry on up the hill onto Barley Lane and reception is on your right.

Rye Bay Caravan Park `7`
Level Road, Winchelsea Beach, East Sussex, TN36 4NE
Tel: 01797 226340
On the A259 two miles west of Rye in Winchelsea village, take road signed 'Winchelsea Beach'. Site is on the left in about three miles.

Seacote Park `60`
St Bees, Cumbria CA27 0ET
Tel: 01946 822777
www.seacote.com
Leave the M6 at Junction 40 and take the A66 west for approximately 35 miles. Take the A595 towards Whitehaven. Keep on the A595, bypassing the town centre. Go through two sets of traffic lights to a roundabout, which you go straight over. Then take the second right, signposted 'St Bees'. At the T-junction at the top of the hill turn left onto the B5345 towards St Bees. Follow the signs to the beach.

Ravenglass Camping and Caravan Club Site `62`
Ravenglass, Cumbria, CA18 1SR
Tel: 01229 717250
www.siteseeker.co.uk
From the A595 turn west for Ravenglass. The site is signed on the left before entering the village.

Long Beach Estate

ISH MARKET

Achnahaird, Ross-shire

SCOTLAND

John O'Groats, Caithness

SCOTLAND

Highland Cow

Scottish Coastal Ruin

Eilean Donan Castle, Dornie

Fishing Nets

SCOTLAND

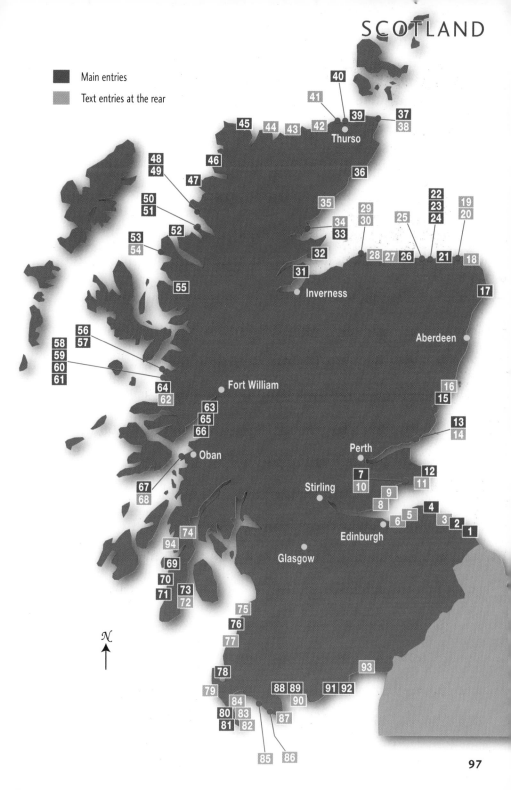

SCOTLAND

Main entries

Text entries at the rear

Thurso

Inverness

Aberdeen

Fort William

Oban

Perth

Stirling

Edinburgh

Glasgow

𝒩

97

SCOTLAND

Thorntonloch Caravan Park [1]

Innerwick, Dunbar, East Lothian,
EH42 1QS
Tel: 01368 840236

Right on its own beautiful surfing beach, this site mostly accommodates static caravans. Ten touring pitches are set aside all with hard standings, a standpipe close by and electric hook-up. The toilet blocks and whole site is immaculately kept. There are beautiful views of the coastline and it is adjacent to a soft sandy beach with surfers providing visual entertainment.

NA	1¹/₂	NP	10	6 AMP		
WC					MG	MB

Pub 7 miles. Shop 3 miles. Small boats from beach.

£££

Directions: Seven miles south of Dunbar on A1, signed 'Thorntonloch', site in 400m.

GPS: N55°57.778'W002°23.988'
OS grid: 67 NT 751 745

March - October

Dunbar Camping and Caravanning Club Site [2]

Oxwellmains, Dunbar, East Lothian,
EH42 1WG Tel: 01368 866881
www.siteseeker.co.uk

Library Picture

This purpose built site opened in September 2008 with all new facilities and amenities. There are views of the sea from most of the site and pitches. The sea is about an eight minute walk. Dunbar town about seven miles away has several places to eat out. A wildlife reserve and a geological trail are also located nearby.

NA		NP	90	10 AMP		
WC					MG	MB

Shop at Dunbar.

£££

Directions: Do not drive through Dunbar. From the A1 southeast of Dunbar, take the A1087 beside the cement works. Travel 500m, going straight over the cement works roundabout, and turn first right, signposted to the campsite. Travel 900m down the single-track road to the campsite.

GPS: N55°59.693'W002°28.812'
OS grid: 67 NT 700 780

April - November

Tantallon Caravan and Camping Park

North Berwick, East Lothian, EH39 5NJ
Tel: 01620 893348
www.meadowhead.co.uk

Overlooking the Firth of Forth from an elevated position, this is truly a magnificent spot. The campsite is level, and spreads across several acres. Static caravans occupy one side of the site and tourers the other. There is masses of space, and most pitches have electric hook-ups. All the pitches provide a glorious view of the sea and the fascinating small islands. The Glen Golf Course spreads out in front of the Campsite and 300m footpath takes you across the golf course to the beach.

Pub 750 metres. Shop 5 minute walk to Tesco.

£££

Directions: The site is situated on the A198 Dunbar - North Berwick road one mile past Tantallon Castle.

GPS: N56°03.338'W002°41.433'
OS grid: 67 NT 571 848

March - October

Monturpie

Upper Largo, Near St Andrews,
Fife, KY8 5QS
Tel: 01333 360254 www.monturpie.co.uk

Located on the top of a hill, Monturpie Guest House is a Traditional, stone built farmhouse. Both the campsite and house have terrific views overlooking the Firth of Forth towards Edinburgh and Leith. This adult only campsite is superb and is beautifully cared for, with newly built toilets and showers. 15 minutes walk downhill takes you to a wonderful little village shop. On site there is a coffee shop and licensed restaurant, open Thursday to Sunday.

Pub and shop ¼ mile at Upper Largo.

£££

Directions: From the south, A915 to Upper Largo to St Andrews Road, the site entrance is on the right just past the end of the village.

GPS: N56°13.288'W002°55.203'
OS grid: 59 NO 433 039

March - October

SCOTLAND

Sauchope Links Caravan Park [12]

The Links, Crail, Fife, KY10 3XT
Tel: 01333 450460
www.largoleisure.co.uk

Beautifully maintained with impeccable facilities, the site is mostly level although parts are sloping. There are static caravans and 50 touring pitches some with hard standings, but all with good views, with the front row having an uninterrupted outlook across the rocky shoreline. Within walking distance is the charming town of Crail, with its steep narrow streets, harbour and sandy beach.

NA 20	NP 50	10 AMP		
WC	♿	📶		

Pub 1/2 mile.

£££

Directions: Turn right off the Crail/Balcomie road one mile northeast of Crail.

GPS: N56°15.697'W002°36.793'
OS grid: 59 NO 624 080

Easter - October

Riverview Caravan Park [13]

Marine Drive, Monifieth, Angus,
DD5 4NN Tel: 01382 535471
www.riverview.co.uk

This is a beautifully maintained, 5 1/2 acre, level site. 45 hard standing, serviced pitches are available, most with a view of the sea over hedges. The toilets and showers are impeccably clean, indeed the whole site is well looked after also offering a sauna, steam baths and a gym. Just over a fence there is an enormous expanse of golden beach on the tidal River Tay.

NA 5 1/2	NP 45	10 AMP		
WC	♿	📶		MG

Pub and Shop 5 minutes walk.

£££

Directions: From Dundee on the A930 in Monifieth, take the next turning on the right past Tescos (Reform Street). At the end of the road turn left and then take the next road on the right under the bridge (height 10ft 6in; 3.7m). The site is then signed on the left.

GPS: N56°28.768'W002°48.767'
OS grid: 54 NO 502 321

All Year

Miltonhaven Seaside Caravan Park 15

St. Cyrus, by Montrose, Kincardineshire, DD10 0DL Tel: 01674 850413
www.miltonhaven.co.uk

The Park covers six flat and grassy acres bordered by two streams. The 15 touring pitches are close to the seashore and most have a sea view. Miltonhaven has its own sandy, safe swimming beach, with rock pools adjacent. Bingo on Saturday is a great evening's entertainment. The Coastal Footpath runs directly in front, allowing leisurely walks to the nearby fishing village of Johnshaven.

| NA 6 | NP 15 | 10 AMP |

| WC | | | | | MG | MB |

Dogs allowed but not with tenters.

£££   🐕   ††   M   i   WiFi

Directions: Two miles North of St. Cyrus. At the crossroads of the A92 and the B9120, turn southeast towards the sea. The site is on the right in about half a mile.

GPS: N56°46.830'W002°22.377'
OS grid: 45 NO 775 655

April - September

Lido Caravan Park 17

South Road, Peterhead, Aberdeenshire, AB42 2YP Tel: 01779 473358
www.aberdeenshire.gov.uk/caravanparks

This is a very good local authority site. The sea views are occupying as you look over Peterhead harbour with its storage tank installations. Sailing and windsurfing are popular in the bay. The site is extremely well cared for and has plenty of benches and picnic tables. The site is well located right next to its own little soft sandy beach and, close to the town, and the lido.

| NA 4 | NP 26 | 10 AMP |

| WC | | | | | MG | MB |

Slipway adjacent.

£££   🐕   ††   M   i   WiFi

Directions: In Peterhead on the seafront by the lido.

GPS: N57°29.790'W001°47.842'
OS grid: 30 NK 123 453

March - October

SCOTLAND

Blackpots Cottages CS `21`

Whitehills, By Banff,
Aberdeenshire, AB45 2JN
Tel: 01261 861396

This small, level, lawned paddock provides terrific sea views. The site is surrounded by a low stone wall which obscures the adjacent road from view when looking out across to the narrow rocky beach to the sea. There is a fishmongers and a fish and chip shop in the village.

| NA | 0.75 | NP | 5 | 0 AMP |

Beach adjacent. Slipway in village.

£££

Directions: Directions: Travel one mile west from Banff on the A98 and turn right onto the B9038 to Whitehills village. At the crossroads turn right, signposted to the harbour. Follow the road to the end of the small peninsula and the CS is on the right past a static park. If heading towards Banff on the A98, turn left on the B9121 two miles before Banff and follow the road for 1¹/₂ miles, passing the harbour, and round to the CS.

GPS: N57°40.823'W002°34.230'
OS grid: 29 NJ 662 658

April - October

Banff Links Caravan Park `22`

Banff, Aberdeenshire, Grampian, AB45 2JJ
Tel: 01261 812228
www.aberdeenshire.gov.uk/caravanparks/locations/banff.asp

Perfectly located, this level site is right next to Banff village with all its amenities. Some static and 28 touring pitches are right on the waterfront on the top of the pebble bank. When the tide is out a large sandy beach is exposed which is great for children, and Boyndie Bay is also a popular surfing spot.

| NA | 3¹/₂ | NP | 62 | 10 AMP |

Slipway at Bannf.

£££

Directions: From Banff, travel west half a mile on the A98 and turn right towards the sea, signposted Banff Links and campsite symbol. Drive in a straight line 500m to the sea and campsite, clearly signposted.

Scottish
TOURIST BOARD
★★★★
HOLIDAY PARK

GPS: N57°40.152'W002°33.210'
OS grid: 29 NJ 673 645

April - October

23 Sandend Caravan Park

Sandend, Portsoy, Aberdeenshire,
AB45 2UA Tel: 01261 842660
www.sandendcaravanpark.co.uk

This site is set in a conservation village and overlooks the gorgeous, flat, golden, sandy beach of Sandend Bay. The site is level throughout but many of the pitches have wonderful sea views and everything is neat, tidy. There is direct access to the beach from site and body boarding will amuse children for hours. Findlater Castle is a short walk away.

NA 4 1/2 NP 48 10 AMP

WC MG MB

Pub 1 mile. Showers 20p.

£££ M WiFi

Directions: Three miles west of Portsoy, turn north off the A98 road to Sandend. The site is on the right in half a mile, adjacent to an old school and a sandy beach.

Scottish Tourist Board ★★★★ Touring Park

GPS: N57°40.930'W002°44.947'
OS grid: 29 NJ 555 661

April - October

24 Cullen Bay Caravan Park

Logie Drive, Cullen, Morayshire, AB56 4TW
Tel: 01542 840766
www.cullenbayholidaypark.co.uk

Cullen Bay Park is neat and well cared for and is located on the edge of the village, just 650m (10 minutes walk) from the centre. The touring pitches, static caravans and some hard standing pitches have interesting sea views across the bay. There are nice coastal walks and bottlenose dolphins are often seen from the cliffs. It takes about 20 minutes to walk to the sea.

NA 5 NP 35 15 AMP

WC MG MB

Pub and shop 10 minutes walk. Slipway at Cullen Harbour.

£££ M WiFi

Directions: Travelling on the A98 through Cullen, turn towards the sea where signed to the campsite. The site is located on the northeast edge of the village beside the playing fields.

Scottish Tourist Board ★★★★ Touring Park

GPS: N57°41.623'W002°48.795'
OS grid: 29 NJ 495 683

April - October

SCOTLAND

Findochty Caravan Park [26]

Jubilee Terrace, Findochty, Buckie, Banffshire,
AB56 4QA Tel: 01542 835303
www.findochtycaravanpark.co.uk

This is a nice compact site built into a rocky hollow looking out over a small shingle beach. The site is conveniently located with a pub next door, and adjacent to the 100 berth harbour of the interesting little town of Findochty. The park is approximately three acres and has mobile homes for hire. There are 30 touring pitches under the cliffs, 20 of which have electric hook-ups. There are good views of the Moray Firth where dolphins are seen almost daily.

NA 3	NP 30	16 AMP		
WC				MG	MB

Pub 4 miles. Slipway 2¹/₂ miles.

££

Directions: Travelling on the A98 halfway between Buckie and Cullen, turn towards the sea on the A928 to Findochty. Travel to the harbour and the site is located on the left-hand side, clearly signed through the village.

GPS: N57°41.890'W002°54.452'
OS grid: 28 NJ 459 679

March - October

Fortrose Caravan Site [31]

Wester Greengates, Fortrose,
Ross-shire, IV10 8RX
Tel: 01381 621927

The site's location on the shoreline of the loch provides interesting, panoramic views across the Moray Firth, including moored sailing craft, the distant hills and a suspension road bridge. This is a beautiful site that is partly level and partly sloping with a quiet road running behind it. A network of footpaths provide for interesting walking around the Black Isle and Chanonry Point where dolphins may be seen.

NA	NP 50	16 AMP		
WC				MG	MB

Shop 10 minute walk. Slipway in harbour.

££

Directions: Off of the A832 to Fortrose. Turn right opposite the Bank of Scotland into Academy Street and the site is on the right in approximately 500m.

GPS: N57°34.723'W004°07.107'
OS grid: 27 NH 734 564

April - September

Rosemarkie Camping and Caravanning Club Site [32]

Ness Road East, Rosemarkie, Fortrose,
Ross-shire, IV10 8SE Tel: 01381 621117
www.siteseeker.co.uk

This is a very attractive level site on the shore of a half-moon bay. There are absolutely beautiful views looking over the Moray and Cromarty Firths. This spectacular coastline is famous for its bottlenose dolphins, which are seen most days from the site. The Fortrose and Rosemarkie golf course is next door. You can walk a short way into a very interesting little town and there is a regular bus service to Inverness.

| NA 6 | NP 60 | 16 AMP | | |

Pub and Shop 10 minutes walk.

£££

Directions: Take the A832 to Fortrose, turning right by the Police Station down Ness Road. Then take the first left into a small turning at the Golf Club sign.

GPS: N57°34.997'W004°06.537'
OS grid: 27 NH 739 569

March - October

Grannie's Helian Hame [33]

Embo, Dornoch, Sutherland,
Highlands, IV25 3QD Tel: 01862 810383
www.parkdeanholidays.co.uk

This large, family site is part of the Parkdean Holidays group and has loads of facilities and entertainment, all set amongst the sand dunes. There is a large play area, adventure playground, indoor heated pool, and bar with entertainment. The spacious touring pitches are located around the edge of the site and many of those with electric hook-ups are right on the edge of the beach. The site is also within walking distance to a small village.

| NA 5 | NP 185 | 13 AMP | | |

Slipway on site.

£££

Directions: From the A9/A949 road to Dornoch, take the unclassified road north for 2¹/₂ miles and turn right into Embo.

GPS: N57°54.463'W003°59.825'
OS grid: 21 NH 818 926

March - October

SCOTLAND

Inver Caravan Park [36]

Houstry Road, Dunbeath, Caithness,
KW6 6EH Tel: 01593 731441
www.inver-caravan-park.co.uk

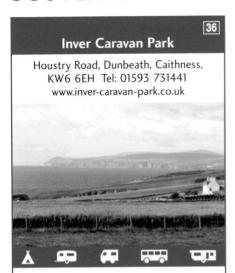

There is a very good sea view from the front row of this site and there are also good views towards the hills. This is a small, well kept site with simple, but good facilities. It is situated quite high above the sea, a 5-10 minute walk down a rather steep path leads to the beach. A longer walk of about a quarter of a mile will give you an easier descent. The beach is rather pebbly with interesting rock pools to explore. Puffins can be seen from walks up the Dunbeath Strath.

| NA 1 | NP 15 | 🔌 16 AMP | | |

| WC | | | | 🔲 | MG | MB |

Pub 350 metres. Shop ¹/₂ mile. Slipway in village.

£££ 🐕 ᵻᵻ M (i) WiFi

Directions: The site is situated on the A9 just north of Dunbeath. The site entrance is 50m up the road towards Houstry.

GPS: N58°15.025'W003°25.267'
OS grid: 11 ND 166 299

All Year

John O'Groats [37]
Camping and Caravan Site

John O'Groats, Caithness, Highlands,
KW1 4YR Tel: 01955 611329
www.johnogroatscampsite.co.uk

This site is right in the heart of the action, but once pitched on the well kept grass you can relax and enjoy panoramic views of the Pentland Firth, one of the most dangerous shipping channels in the world with spectacular tidal races. You can also see the Island of Stroma, the Orkney Islands, and Duncansby Head Lighthouse. Grey seals are often seen swimming close to the beach.

| NA 4 | NP 90 | 🔌 16 AMP | | |

| WC | | | | 🔲 | MG | MB |

Pub adjacent. Shop ¹/₂ mile. Slipway John O'Groats. RV's 2.

£££ 🐕 ᵻᵻ M (i) WiFi

Directions: Situated at the end of the A99.

GPS: N58°38.613'W003°04.115'
OS grid: 7 ND 383 731

April - September

Dunnet Bay Caravan Club Site [39]

Dunnet, Thurso, Highland, KW14 8XD
Tel: 01847 821319
www.caravanclub.co.uk

Many pitches have glorious views of the sea through sand dunes, and some are right next to the beach. Solitude can be enjoyed here whilst you look out over uninterrupted clean washed sands to Dunnet Head, the northernmost point of mainland of Britain. Climbing Dunnet will reward you with magnificent views over the Pentland Firth to Orkney, Ben Loyal and Ben Hope. Units over 28 feet should contact site in advance.

| NA | 5 | | NP | 57 | | 16 AMP | | |

Pub 1/2 mile. Shop 21/2 miles. Boats can be launched from beach.

£££

Directions: Travelling from the east (John O'Groats) on the A836, the site is located on the right, half a mile past Dunnet village. Travelling from the west (Thurso) on the A836, the site is located on the left 21/2 miles past Castletown village.

GPS: N58°36.927'W003°20.672'
OS grid: 12 ND 219 705

April - October

West Murkle CL [40]

1 West Murkle, Thurso, Caithness, Highlands, KW14 8YT Tel: 01847 896405
www.caithnesshost.co.uk/WestMurkle

Nestled between Thurso Bay and Dunnet Bay lies Murkle where this wonderful little Caravan Club CL is located. Unfortunately, only two pitches enjoy sea views, but the sand and pebble beach is an easy two hundred yard walk away. This is great place for a few days tranquillity away from the hustle and bustle of the modern world.

| NA | 1/4 | | NP | 5 | | 0 AMP | | |

Pub and Shop 2 minutes at Castledown.

£££

Directions: Turn right off the A9 at Thurso onto the A836, signposted 'Castletown'. After 23/4 miles turn left, signposted 'West Murkle'. Within one mile, turn right at a T-junction. After half a mile turn right through a gate onto a gravel road. Cross the field to a second cattle grid gate and the site is on your left.

GPS: N58°36.403'W003°26.425'
OS grid: 12 ND 165 693

All Year

SCOTLAND

Sango Sands Caravan and Camping Site [45]

Durness, Sutherland, Highlands, IV27 4PZ
Tel: 01971 511726
www.sangosands.com

This is a large, sprawling site and you are allowed to find any little nook and cranny to pitch on. You can even park on the cliff edge with a sheer drop to the sea below. The ground is partly level and partly sloping. The sandy bay is edged by rocky cliffs and the nearby islands make this bay ideal for snorkelling and body boarding. The beaches are a one minute walk away.

| NA 10 | NP 104 | ☠ 16 AMP | 🔌 | 🔌 |
| WC | ♿ | 🚿 | | ⚱ | ⭕ | MG | MB |

⚑ 🧺 ⍾ ⚓ ☒ 🛝 🚶

Shop 200 metres.

£££ 🐕 🚻 M ⓘ WiFi

Directions: Adjacent to the A838 in Durness village overlooking Sango Bay.

GPS: N58°34.108'W004°44.603'
OS grid: 09 NC 405 678

April - October

Scourie Caravan and Camping Park [46]

Harbour Road, Lairg, Sutherland, Highlands, IV27 4TG
Tel: 01971 502060 (No bookings taken)

This four acre site provides a good view of the bay. The 60 pitches are on level ground with some on hard standings. The site has excellent facilities, is well laid out, very tidy and close to the shops and the beach. The water is exceptionally clear, making it ideal for skin diving. Golden eagles, deer, otters, badgers, wildcats and pine martins can be seen in the nearby hilly walking country. Seals can also be seen locally. No advanced bookings are taken for this site, just turn up.

| NA 4 | NP 75 | ☠ 5-13 AMP | 🔌 | 🔌 |
| WC | ♿ | 🚿 | | ⚱ | ⭕ | MG | MB |

⚑ 🧺 ⍾ ⚓ ☒ 🛝 🚶

Slipway 200 metres.

£££ 🐕 🚻 M ⓘ WiFi

Directions: On the A894 in Scourie, overlooking Scourie Bay. 26 miles from Durness and 45 miles from Ullapool.

GPS: N58°21.088'W005°09.313'
OS grid: 09 NC 154 446

April - September

Shore Caravan Site **47**

106 Achmelvich, Lochinver, Sutherland,
Highlands, IV27 4JB Tel: 01571 844393
www.shorecaravansite.yolasite.com

This is an attractive site with plenty of space. The pitches are partly level, partly sloping with some hard standings. The seascape almost looks Mediterranean, and the silver sand in the bay and the flotilla of small craft all add to the ambience. No advanced bookings are taken, just turn up, and relax.

| NA | 6 | NP | 60 | 16 AMP | | |

| WC | | | | | | MG | MB |

Slipway 4¹/₂ miles at Lochinver.

£££   M ⓘ WiFi

Directions: Travelling on the A837, half a mile before Lochinver, turn right onto the B869, signposted 'Stoer', 'Drumbeg', 'Achmelvich'. In 1¹/₂ miles turn left, signposted 'Achmelvich', for 1¹/₂ miles. In the village, go past the telephone box straight onto the site, about 250 yards down at the end of the road.

GPS: N58°10.138'W005°18.427'
OS grid: 15 NC 055 248

April - October

Ardmair Point Caravan Park **48**

Ardmair Point, Ullapool, Ross-shire,
IV26 2TN Tel: 01854 612054
www.ardmair.com

Occupying a small peninsula with a curved pebble bay, this site is set amongst spectacular Highland scenery with the dramatic Ben Mhor Coigach mountain ridge as the backdrop for the sheltered sea loch. There is self-catering accommodation, as well as touring and camping pitches, all with spectacular views and great facilities nearby.

| NA | 8 | NP | 50 | 10 AMP | | |

| WC | | | | | | MG | MB |

Pub 3 miles. Boat launching from site.

£££   M ⓘ WiFi

Directions: Three miles north of Ullapool on the A835, look for a campsite sign by a telephone box.

GPS: N57°56.022'W005°11.787'
OS grid: 19 NH 109 983

April - September

Broomfield Holiday Park 49

West Lane, Ullapool, Ross-shire, IV26 2UT
Tel: 01854 612020
www.broomfieldhp.com

Right on the banks of Lochbroom, this site offers lovely views of the Summer Islands and the Hebrides. Situated in an outstanding environment with wonderful scenery and amazing sunsets, but is conveniently located right next to Ullapool. There is still a major fishing fleet in Ullapool, so visitors can enjoy the comings and goings of the boats and the bounty that they bring home.

| NA | 11 | NP | 140 | 16 AMP | |
| WC | | | | MG | MB |

Slipway in town.

£££

Directions: In Ullapool, continue along Shore Street and take the second right after the harbour where you will see a wide site entrance on the left.

GPS: N57°53.657'W005°09.887'
OS grid: 19 NH 125 938

Easter - September

Northern Lights 50

Croft 9, Badcaul, Dundonnell,
Ross-shire, IV23 2QY
Tel: 07786 274175 / 01697 371379

This wonderful little six acre site is kept neat and tidy and well mown. There is room for 12 touring caravans, motorhomes or tents with some hard standings. The facilities are housed in a sympathetically refurbished old stone building. Access to sandy beaches is about four miles away. Being surrounded by hills TV reception is very poor, but makes for a dramatic sea and landscape.

| NA | 6 | NP | 12 | 10 AMP | |
| WC | | | | MG | MB |

Pub 4 miles. Shop 1/2 mile. Showers 50p.

£££

Directions: From Inverness, follow the signs to Ullapool and take the A835 until you reach the Braemore Junction. Turn left onto the A832, following signs for Dundonnell, Aultbea, and Gairloch. Follow the road for approximately 19 miles. You will pass the Dundonnell Hotel on your left. The site is four miles past hotel on your right.

GPS: N57°52.060'W005°20.078'
OS grid: 19 NH 024 914

April - September

51 Badrallach

Croft 9, Badrallach, Dundonnell,
Ross-shire, IV23 2QP
Tel: 01854 633281 www.badrallach.com

This is a small family run site situated in a beautiful and tranquil setting. The owners are romantic about the remoteness and still offer spring water and gas lights. The sea view is only partial once pitched, but they are very fine from the shore or the road. There is no chemical disposal point or TV reception. There are 12 tent pitches and three caravan pitches on request.

NA	45	NP	15	16 AMP		
WC					MG	MB

Pub 8 miles. Shop 14 miles. Walkers welcome.

£££

Directions: Turn left off the A835 at Braemar Junction (12 miles south of Ullapool) onto the A832. After 11 miles turn right at the sign for Badralloch and follow the single track road for about eight miles. The site is on the left.

GPS: N57°52.407'W005°15.722'
OS grid: 19 NH 065 915

All Year

52 Gruinard Bay Caravan Park

Laide, Wester Ross, Highlands, IV22 2ND
Tel: 01445 731225
www.gruinard.scotshost.co.uk

This is a small, well cared for, family run site that is Is beachside in the village of Laide. The ruins of the Chapel of Sand are adjacent to the park and, along with the uninterrupted sea views, add real atmosphere to the setting. You can walk two miles down a track from Laide to the ruins of Slaggan, where there is also a superb beach.

NA	3¹/₂	NP	40	10 AMP		
WC					MG	MB

Pub 2¹/₂ miles. Slipway 1 mile.

£££

Directions: The site is situated on the A832 (Gairloch/Ullapool) road just past the village of Laide.

GPS: N57°51.997'W005°32.193'
OS grid: 19 NG 906 918

April - October

Scottish
TOURIST BOARD
★★★★
CAMPING
PARK

SCOTLAND

Gairloch Caravan and Camping Holiday Park `53`

Mihol Road, Strath, Gairloch, Wester Ross, Highlands, IV21 2BX Tel: 01445 712373
www.gairlochcaravanpark.com

The park looks out to the Isle of Skye and west to the outer Hebrides. Across the loch lie the mountains of the Torridon Forest, creating a magnificent landscape. All sorts of amenities are right on the doorstep and the sea is just across the road. There are some hard standing pitches, two static caravans and a cottage for hire.

| NA 10 | NP 63 | 16 AMP | | |

| WC | | | | |

Shop adjacent. Slipway 2 miles.

£££   🐕   ‍‍   M   ⓘ   WiFi

Directions: Turn west off the A832 in Gairloch onto the B8021. After half a mile turn right immediately after the Millcroft Hotel, the site is on your right.

Scottish TOURIST BOARD ★★★★ TOURING PARK

GPS: N57°43.883'W005°42.172'
OS grid: 19 NG 797 774

April - October

Shieldaig Camping Area `55`

Shieldaig Village, Ross-shire, IV54 8XW

This is a village grazing area where camping is permitted. It is a beautiful spot and the exceptional environment should be well respected. There are superb views over Lochs Shieldaig and Torridon, often with beautiful sunsets. Being unsupervised and unserviced except for a water tap, campers are trusted to donate about £5 in the honesty box.

| NA 1/2 | NP 20 | 0 AMP | | |

Slipway in village.

£££   🐕   ‍‍   M   ⓘ   WiFi

Directions: The site is situated in Shieldaig village off the A896 between Lochcarron and Kinlochewe. From the south, leave the A896 at the second sign for the village. The site is on the left in 400m.

GPS: N57°31.530'W005°38.878'
OS grid: 24 NG 816 542

April - October

Invercaimbe Caravan and Camping Site
56

Arisaig, Inverness-shire, PH39 4NT
Tel: 01687 450375
www.invercaimbecaravansite.co.uk

Photo campsite owner

Invercaimbe is a West Highland working croft where traditional hill cattle and working highland ponies have been bred for 150 years. It is a lovely little site spread across a couple of acres, most of which is uneven. It is best to check before booking to make sure that a suitable pitch is available. This is a nice, basic site with wild views of the mountains behind it and a lovely safe beach in front. Boat trips can be taken to all the Inner Hebridean islands.

NA	2	NP	20	10 AMP

Pub 1/2 mile. Shop 1 mile.

££

Directions: From the A830 Fort William-Mallaig road, turn left onto the B8008 at Arisaig. The site is signed on the left in approximately one mile.

GPS: N56°55.638'W005°51.552'
OS grid: 40 NM 652 883

Easter - October

Camusdarach Campsite
57

Camusdarach, Arisaig, Inverness-shire,
PH39 4NT Tel: 01687 450221
www.camusdarach.com

Managed in an environmentally responsible manner and with absolutely pristine facilities, this site is lovely despite only having partial sea views. The grounds are very well cared for and large mature trees provide excellent shelter. A footpath from the site gives access to the superb sandy beaches, which are a mere three minute stroll away. The beach is also licensed for weddings.

NA	NP	42	16 AMP

Pub 3 miles. Shop 4 miles.

££

Directions: From the A830 Fort William-Mallag road, turn left onto the B8008 at Arisaig. The site is signed in approximately four miles on the left.

GPS: N56°57.262'W005°50.782'
OS grid: 40 NM 654 894

March - October

The Croft `[58]`

"Back of Keppoch" Arisaig, Inverness-shire,
PH39 4NS
Tel: 01687 450200

This is a slightly sloping site with basic facilities. However, it is in a wonderful part of the world, in an interesting sandy and rocky bay. The views are very beautiful and, being west facing, there could be spectacular sunsets. There is direct access to the sandy beach and its rocky outcrops and rock pools.

NA 3   NP 15   10 AMP

WC

Pub 1/2 mile. Shop 1 1/2 miles.

£££   M   (i)   WiFi

Directions: From the A830 Fort William-Mallag road, turn left onto the B8008 at Arisaig. Turn left at the 'Back of Keppoch' sign and follow the road for half a mile. The site entrance is signed on the right.

GPS: N56°55.398'W005°51.548'
OS grid: 40 NM 647 881

Easter - October

Silversands Caravan Site `[59]`

Portnaluchaig, Inverness,
PH39 4NT
Tel: 01687 450269

Nicely mown and level, this is a lovely little site but the facilities are basic. Pitches are distributed in little nooks and crannies all over the site, providing seclusion for those who want it. Access to the sea and rock pools is only a short walk away. Campers really love this site, and it can be very busy at weekends.

NA   NP 18   0 AMP

WC

Pub 2 miles. Shop 2 1/2 miles.

£££   M   (i)   WiFi

Directions: From the A830 Fort William-Mallag road, turn left onto the B8008 at Arisaig. The site is on the left in 2 1/2 miles, next to the Caravan Club CL.

GPS: N56°56.362'W005°51.480'
OS grid: 40 NM 653 898

March - October

60
Gorten Sands Caravan Site

Gorten Farm, Arisaig, Inverness-shire,
Highlands, PH39 4NS
Tel: 01687 450283

Next to a white sandy beach, this is a very small and pleasant site with good facilities and wonderful views. The shoreline is rocky and should make for interesting snorkelling and fishing. The campsite is part of the Macdonald family working hill and coastal farm, where traditional harvesting methods are still employed.

| NA 6 | NP 45 | 6 AMP | | |
| WC | | | | □ | MG | MB |

Pub 3/4 mile. Shop 2 miles. Small boats on site.

£££

Directions: From the A830 Fort William-Mallaig road, turn left onto the B8008 at Arisaig. Turn left at the 'Back of Keppoch' sign and follow the road for approximately one mile to the end, where you will find the site entrance.

Scottish TOURIST BOARD
★★★★
TOURING PARK

GPS: N56°55.398'W005°51.548'
OS grid: 40 NM 643 878

May - September

61
Portnadoran Caravan Site

Arisaig, Inverness-shire,
PH39 4NT
Tel: 01687 450267

© Audrey MacDonald

The site is right on the edge of a soft, white sandy beach interspersed with rocks. There are stunning views as the site overlooks the Isles of Skye, Eigg, Rhum and Muck. It is a wonderful, informally managed, commercial site that people return to year after year. Porpoises and otters are seen locally and kids will love the rock pooling. Small boats can be launched from site.

| NA 4 | NP 40 | 10 AMP | | |
| WC | | | | □ | MG | |

Pub 1/2 mile. Shop 2 miles. Showers 20p.

£££

Directions: From the A830 Fort William-Mallag road, turn left onto the B8008 at Arisaig. The site is signed on the left in approximately two miles.

GPS: N56°55.977'W005°51.643'
OS grid: 40 NM 650 891

April - October

SCOTLAND

Bunree Caravan Club Site [63]

Onich, Fort William, PH33 6SE
Tel: 01855 821283
www.caravanclub.co.uk

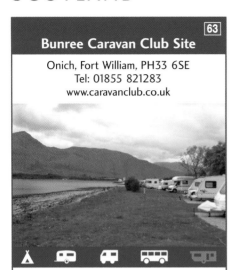

This site is located on the water's edge of Loch Linnhe and has sea and mountain views. This is a very attractive Caravan Club site and non-members are welcome. Mature trees give a wonderful natural feel to this well managed site. The bus to Fort William stops 300m from site. Travelling between Glencoe and Fort William on the A82, half a mile south of the Corran Ferry, by a small bridge, turn towards the sea onto a private road with cattle grid, signed for the site. Follow the road 450m to the sea and site entrance.

| NA | 7 | NP | 99 | 16 AMP | | |
| WC | | | | | | MG | MB |

Shop 1¹/₂ miles.

£££

Directions: Turn left off A82 (Glencoe-Fort William) one mile past Onich at Caravan Club sign on to a narrow track with traffic lights.

GPS: N56°42.925'W005°13.750'
OS grid: 41 NN 019 626

March - January

Traigh CL [64]

Tigh-Na-Bruaich, Arisaig, Inverness,
PH39 4NT Tel: 01687 450645
www.traighgolf.co.uk

Everyone gets a beautiful sea view from this slightly sloping Caravan Club CL and the beach is only a few metres away. This CL is immediately next door to Silversands campsite.

| NA | 1 | NP | 5 | 0 AMP | | |

Pub 2 miles. Shop 2¹/₂ miles Arisaig.

£££

Directions: From the A830 Fort William-Mallag road, turn left onto the B8008 at Arisaig. The site is on the left in 2¹/₂ miles.

GPS: N56°56.362'W005°51.480'
OS grid: 40 NM 654 898

All Year

Seaview Camping and Caravan Park 65

Kielcroft, Benderloch, Oban,
Argyll, PA37 1QS
Tel: 01631 720360

This is a pleasant site with a reasonably level field and some hard standing pitches. It is a lovely, quiet, and peaceful place with views of the bay and hills across the fields. The beach is a short walk away and the site is handy for forest walks and Tralee Rally Carting. Fresh water charges may apply.

NA	4	NP	40	16 AMP		
WC					MG	MB

Pub 2 miles. Shop ¹/₂ mile.

£££ M WiFi

Directions: Turn right off the A85 Oban/Connell road onto the A828 and cross Connell bridge, signposted 'Fort William'. In three miles, just past Benderloch village, turn left into the road signposted 'South Shian/Tralee'. The site is 550m on the left .

GPS: N56°29.780'W005°24.648'
OS grid: 49 NM 901 387

April - September

North Ledaig Caravan Club Site 66

Connel, Oban, Argyll and Bute, PA37 1RU
Tel: 01631 710291
www.caravanclub.co.uk

© Tony Hardley

This 30 acre park is situated alongside a two mile sand and shingle beach. Ardmucknish Bay is perfect for sailing and other water sports and provides safe bathing. Some of the pitches are almost at the water's edge and all pitches face the sea and enjoy a panoramic view across to the beautiful Isle of Mull. The site is ideal for children and has an adventure playground adjacent.

NA	30	NP	280	10 AMP		
WC					MG	MB

Pub 1 mile.

£££ M WiFi

Directions: From Oban head 4 miles northeast on the A85, turn right, just before Connel Bridge, onto the A828, signposted 'Fort William'. This will take you over Connel Bridge, which is restricted to 13.6" - 4.2m. Continue one mile north on the A828 and the site is clearly visible on the left.

Scottish
TOURIST BOARD
★★★★★
TOURING
PARK

GPS: N56°28.660'W005°23.935'
OS grid: 49 NM 907 368

Easter - October

SCOTLAND

Oban Caravan and Camping park [67]

Gallanachmore Farm, Gallanch Road, Oban, Argyll, PA34 4QH Tel: 01631 562425
www.obancaravanpark.com

Superb for all campers, this nine acre site is part of a working farm, set alongside the coast road and overlooking the Sound of Kerrera. This is a very interesting and attractive, mainly level site with some hard standings and very helpful staff. There are beautiful views all around and it is a very nice place to visit with masses to do. This is great walking country, and the sea is a few minutes walk.

NA 9   NP 150   0 AMP

Pub and shops 2¹/₂ miles.

£££

Directions: From Oban town centre follow the signposts to Gallanach. The site is 2¹/₂ miles along the coast road.

GPS: N56°23.395'W005°31.010'
OS grid: 49 NM 830 272

April - September

Point Sands Holiday Park [69]

Tayinloan, Argyll, PA29 6XG
Tel: 01583 441263
www.pointsands.co.uk

A level site right on the sea where you can pitch directly next to the soft sandy beach. There are absolutely superb views over the bay to the Isles of Gigha, Islay, and Jura. The children's play area is unfenced in the camping field. The long sandy beach offers safe bathing, sailing, windsurfing and other water sports.

NA 16   NP 80   16 AMP   MG   MB

Pub 1 mile. Showers 50p.

£££

Directions: 17 miles south of Tarbert on the A83 Campbeltown road. The site is one mile down a drive on the seashore.

GPS: N55°40.320'W005°38.960'
OS grid: 62 NR 698 484

April - October

Muasdale Holiday Park   70

Muasdale, Tarbert, Argyll, PA29 6XD
Tel: 01583 421207
www.muasdaleholidays.com

© Alison Clements

This two acre site split in two with statics on one side and tourers and tents the other. Pitches are narrow and tents over 12 feet will require two pitches. Since the site is right beside the beach, you can jump from your pitch onto the soft white sand and will enjoy beautiful views of the islands. This is an ideal location if you are looking for peace and tranquillity, and it is convenient for ferries to Arran, Gigha, Islay and Jura.

NA 2   NP 15   10 AMP

WC   MG   MB

Pub 4 miles. Shop in village 100 metres. Slipway Tayinloan.

£££   M   WiFi

Directions: From the M8 in Glasgow, signposted 'Erskine Bridge', cross the bridge and pick up the A82 towards Crianlarich and Loch Lomond. Continue to Tarbert and pick up the A83 towards Campbeltown. Continue through Inveraray, Lochgilphead and Tarbet (Loch Fyne). Muasdale is 22 miles south of Tarbert and 15 miles north of Campbeltown.

GPS: N55°35.873'W005°41.148'
OS grid: 68 NR 678 399

Easter - Mid October

Killegruer Caravan Site   71

Woodend, Glenbarr, Tarbert,
Argyll, PA29 6XB
Tel: 01583 421241

© Anne Littleson

The site is mostly occupied with static caravans, but there are 20 touring pitches right next to the beach. This is a nice, comfortable, tidy site isolated right on the west coast of the Kintyre Peninsula. The beach is sandy and interspersed with rocks, but body boarding should be possible. The site is within reasonable driving distance of Campbeltown.

NA 4   NP 20   16 AMP

WC   MG   MB

Pub 1 mile. Shop 1/2 mile. Slipway 5 miles Tayinloan.

£££   M   WiFi

Directions: Turn right off the A83 one mile south of Glenbarr village. 12 miles from Campbeltown.

GPS: N55°33.363'W005°42.418'
OS grid: 68 NR 663 352

April - October

SCOTLAND

73
Carradale Bay Caravan Park

Carradale, Cambeltown, Argyll, PA28 6QG
Tel: 01583 431665
www.carradalebay.com

© Colin Burgess

The park is alonside a one mile long, south facing sandy beach backed by dunes. Landscaping provides small camping areas protected by shrubs and bushes, each pitch having good sea views across to the Isle of Arran. Situated in an area of outstanding natural beauty, this site is suitable for families as there is plenty of walking and cycling in the adjacent Forestry Commission land.

NA	NP 90	10 AMP		
WC				

Pub 15 minutes. Shop 1 mile.

£££

Directions: The site is located off the B842, halfway between Claonaig and Campbeltown. Follow the single-track road 600m to the sea and the site entrance, clearly signed. Large units should approach on the A38 to Campbeltown then the B842 towards Carradale.

GPS: N55°35.218'W005°29.482'
OS grid: 69 NR 803 373

Easter - September

Culzean Castle Camping 76
and Caravanning Club Site

Culzean, Maybole, Ayrshire, KA19 8JX
Tel: 01655 760627
www.siteseeker.co.uk

The site is in the grounds of the magnificent Culzean Castle with good views across arable fields to the sea. The mountains of the Isle of Arran litter the horizon, creating spectacular sunsets. The sea is about a 2¹/₂ mile drive away. A range of events are held at Culzean Castle, which is open to the public.

NA 600	NP 90	10 AMP		
WC				

Pub 4 miles. Slipway 2¹/₂ miles.

£££

Directions: From the A77 Girvan to Maybole road, at Turnbury, take the A719. The site is signed on the left in approximately three miles.

GPS: N55°21.213'W004°46.180'
OS grid: 70 NS 247 099

March - October

Hillhead of Craichmore CL [78]

Leswalt, Stranraer,
Dumfriesshire & Galloway, DG9 0PN
Tel: 01776 870219

Enclosed within stonewalls and trees, lies an attractive, fairly level, traditional, and peaceful CL. with fine views across the Loch Ryan. You can sit and watch ferries going to and from Stranraer and it is only about a quarter of a mile to the shingle beach.

NA 1/4   NP 5   10 AMP

WC   MG   MB

Pub 3 miles. Shop Stranraer. Slipway 1 1/2 miles.

£££   M   WiFi

Directions: Leave Stranraer on the A718 Stranraer-Kirkcolm road. In two miles turn right at the roundabout and in about a quarter of a mile turn right into the farm road.

GPS: N54°55.873'W005°04.290'
OS grid: 82 NX 033 640

All Year

Ardwell Caravan Park [80]

Luce View Cottage, Ardwell,
Dumfries & Galloway, DG9 9LS
Tel: 01776 860230

This is a very pleasant, simple, level site with superb views of the Irish Sea and Luce Bay. Pitches are on the water's edge with firm ground, and a hardcore road runs through the site. Facilities onsite are basic and site fees are inexpensive.

NA   NP 25   0 AMP

WC   MG   MB

Shop at Sandhead. Slipway 1/2 mile.

£££   M   WiFi

Directions: From Glenluce, take the A7084 to Ardwell. Look carefully for the site notice on the right towards the end of the village.

GPS: N54°46.245'W004°56.457'
OS grid: 82 NX 108 456

March - October

SCOTLAND

Muldaddie Farm House CL

Port Logan, Stranraer, DG9 9NJ
Tel: 01776 860212
www.caravanclub.co.uk

This is a slightly sloping site on a cliff edge overlooking the bay and Port Logan. It is a very clean and tidy site with good access to the sea and beautiful panoramic views across the bay. Port Logan is only a short walk away and has a small harbour and a pub.

| NA | 2 | NP | 5 | | 16 AMP | | |

| WC | | | | | | MG | MB |

Pub, shop and beach 1/2 mile.

£££   M   (i)   WiFi

Directions: From Stranrear travel two miles south on the A77,contine straight on where the road becomes the A716 for a further nine miles. Turn right onto the B7065, signposted 'Port Logan two miles'. Travel through Port Logan and the site is just past village hall up a dead end road.

GPS: N54°43.277'W004°57.700'
OS grid: 82 NX 093 403

Easter - September

Mossyard Caravan Park

Gatehouse of Fleet, Castle Douglas,
Dumfries and Galloway, DG7 2ET
Tel: 01557 840226 www.mossyard.co.uk

This is a 6 1/2 acre, mostly level, nicely mown site with sea views from most pitches. Indeed, some pitches lay very close to the rocky and sandy shore. The site is part of the McConchie family working farm who have welcomed campers for three generations. Thanks to its wide open, grassy areas, this beautiful and exceptionally well maintained site offers visitors a great feeling of space.

| NA | 6 1/2 | NP | 36 | | 10 AMP | | |

| WC | | | | | | MG | MB |

Shop 1 mile. Showers 20p.

£££   M   (i)   WiFi

Directions: Three quarters of a mile off the A75 west of Gatehouse of Fleet.

GPS: N54°50.433'W004°15.625'
OS grid: 83 NX 550 516

March - October

Auchenlarie Holiday Park **89**

Gatehouse of Fleet, Dumfries and Galloway,
DG7 2EX Tel: 01556 506200
www.auchenlarie.co.uk

This is a very large, beautifully maintained holiday park with extensive excellent facilities making it a high quality, all singing and all dancing holiday destination. The touring area is high up with beautiful sea views. Hard standings are available all of which are level and there are also some Super pitches. The site has its own sandy, sheltered cove reached by a wide, gravel, and gently sloping cliff path.

NA		NP 70	16 AMP		
WC					MG	MB

Shop at Sandhead. Slipway 1/2 mile.

£££

Directions: From Dumfries follow the A75 Stranraer until the sign 'Gatehouse of Fleet'. Continue past the town for five miles and the holiday park is on the left.

GPS: N54°50.629'W004°16.814'
OS grid: 83 NX 536 522

All Year

Castle Point Caravan Site **91**

Rockcliffe, By Dalbeattie,
Dumfries and Galloway, DG5 4QL
Tel: 01556 630248

Real Scottish sea, islands and mountain views are enjoyed from the site, which is very well maintained, clean and tidy. A fairly steep and rough path takes you to a small cove near Castle Point. The 10 minute walk to the point has exciting views of the sea and there are good walks in the area and a safe interesting beach in the village, about one mile away.

NA 3		NP 15	16 AMP		
WC					MG	MB

Pub 1/2 mile. Shop 1 mile.

£££

Directions: From Dalbeattie take the A710 coastal road. After five miles turn right along the road signposted to 'Rockcliffe'. At the brow of the hill just on entering Rockcliffe turn left and drive down to the end of Barclay Road and straight ahead up a private farm road.

GPS: N54°51.565'W003°47.065'
OS grid: 84 NX 855 532

Easter - October

SCOTLAND

Sandyhills Bay Leisure Park

Sandyhills, Dalbeattie, Dumfries and
Galloway, DG5 4NY Tel: 01387 780257
www.gillespie-leisure.co.uk

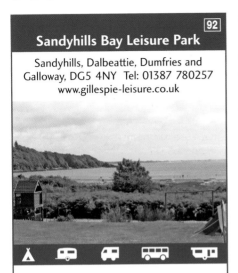

This is a really attractive site that is professionally
maintained. It is ideal for families and has a useful shop
and good facilities. The long sandy beach is directly
accessible from the site and has a good tidal range, and
even some salt marsh. The bay provides safe swimming
and the wooded hill provides a harmonious backdrop
to the site. The area is dotted with smugglers' coves
which are accessible at low tide.

NA	4		NP	54		16 AMP		

Pub and shop 5 minutes.

£££

Directions: Take the A710 coast road from Dalbeattie
to Dumfries. The site is on the right at Sandyhills
village just past the golf course.

GPS: N54°52.795'W003°43.852'
OS grid: 84 NX 890 549

April - October

Thurston Manor Holiday Home Park 3
Innerwick, Dunbar, EH42 1SA
01368 840643
www.thurstonmanor.co.uk
Two miles south of Dunbar on the A1, signposted for
'Innerwick' and 'Crowhill'.

Aberlady Station Caravan Park 5
Haddington Rd, Longniddry, East Lothian, EH32 0PZ
Tel: 01875 870666
From Haddington take the A6137 for about 4¹/₂ miles
to Aberlady. The site is on the left quite close to the
village and close to the sea.

Seton Sands Holiday Village 6
Longniddry, East Lothian, EH32 0QF
Tel: 08712 310867
www.haven.com
Take the A1 as far as the Tranent slip road. Turn onto
the B6371 for Cockenzie and then turn right onto the
B1348. The site is in one mile, on the right, clearly
signposted.

Pettycur Bay Caravan Park 8
Burntisland Road, Kinghorn, Fife, KY3 9YE
Tel: 01592 892200
www.pettycur.co.uk
Half a mile west of Kinghorn on the A921. The site is
well signed.

Leven Beach Holiday Park 9
North Promenade, Leven, Fife, KY8 4HY
Tel: 01333 426008
www.pettycur.co.uk/levenbeach.asp
Find the north end of Leven promenade and follow
signs for the caravan site.

Woodland Gardens Caravan and Camping Site 10
Blindwell Road, Lundin Links, by Leven, Fife, KY8 5QG
Tel: 01333 360319
www.woodland-gardens.co.uk
Turn north of the A915 Kirkcaldy - Leven - St Andrews
road at the east end of Lundin Links.

Shell Bay Caravan Park 11
Shell Bay, Elie, Fife, KY9 1HB
Tel: 01333 330283
www.abbeyfordscotland.com/shellbay.html

---

1 1/2 miles northwest of Elie, turn off the A917 and follow the road to Shell Bay. This is a single track road but there are passing places. The site is well signed.

Tayview Holiday Park 14
Marine Drive, Monifieth, Dundee, DD5 4NL
Tel: 01382 532837
www.tayview.info
Exit the A92 halfway between Dundee and Arbroath onto the B962 south. In the centre of Monifieth, turn left into the parade of shops, signposted 'seafront golf courses' and 'Riverside Caravan Park'. Drive 250m, turning left at the railway track and then right under the railway (3.2m, 10.6ft). Drive through the parking area and follow the coast on the left to the site entrance.

Wairds Park Caravan Site 16
Beach Road, Johnshaven, Montrose, Angus, DD10 0EP
Tel: 01561 362395
On the A92 road nine miles north of Montrose. Turn right at the Johnshaven signpost. Follow the road to the harbour, turning left onto the beach road. Turn right at the T-junction and the site is on your left at the end of the road.

The Esplanade Caravan Park 18
Fraserburgh, Aberdeenshire, AB43 5EU
Tel: 01346 510041
www.aberdeenshire.gov.uk/caravanparks/locations/fraserburgh.asp
Located on the east side of Fraserburgh, between the harbour and beach.

Wester Bonnyton Farm 19
Gamrie, Banff, Grampian, AB45 3EP
Tel: 01261 832470
http://wester-bonnyton.xplodelite.com
On the Banff Fraserburgh Coastal Trail /B9031, two miles east of MacDuff.

Rosehearty Caravan Park 20
The Harbour, Rosehearty, Fraserburgh, Aberdeenshire, AB43 7JQ
Tel: 01346 510041
On the seafront in Rosehearty overlooking the beach.

Portsoy Caravan Park 25
The Links, Portsoy, Aberdeenshire, AB45 2RQ
Tel: 01261 842695
In Portsoy turn north off the A98 to Church Street. In 120 yards turn right into Institute Street. The Caravan Park is on a sheltered bay overlooking the Moray Firth.

Strathlene Caravan Site 27
Great Eastern Road, Strathlene, Portessie, Buckie, Moray, AB56 1SR
Tel: 01224 696479
www.ukparks.co.uk/strathlenecaravan
On the Coastal Trail between Cullen and Buckie. Follow the tourist board signs for Strathlene Caravan Park. From the A98 Cullen to Fochaber road take the A942 Coastal Trail. The caravan site is located at Port Essie between a golf course and Buckie.

Lossiemouth Bay Caravan Site 28
East Beach, Lossiemouth, Moray, Scotland, IV31 6NW
Tel: 01343 813980
www.lossiemouthcaravans.co.uk
Drive into Lossiemouth on the A941 Elgin Road and turn right at the sports ground into Church Street and follow signs for the caravan site. The site is well signed.

Burghead Beach Caravan Park 29
Burghead, Elgin, Moray, IV30 5RP
Tel: 01343 830084
www.lossiemouthcaravans.co.uk/burghead.asp
The site is in Burghead off the B9013 road. Eight miles northwest of Elgin adjacent to a sandy beach.

Station Caravan Park 30
West Beach, Hopeman, Moray, IV30 5RU
Tel: 01343 830880
www.stationcaravanpark.co.uk
In Hopeman off the B9012 road near the harbour.

Dornoch Caravan and Camping Park 34
The Links, Dornoch, Sutherland, IV25 3LX
Tel: 01862 810 423
www.dornochcaravans.co.uk
Travelling north on the A9 towards Thurso, turn right to Dornoch and drive two miles to Dornoch centre. Turn right onto church Street and the site is 400 yards on the right.

SCOTLAND

Greenpark Caravan Site `35`
Brora, Sutherland, KW9 6LP
Tel: 01408 621513
On the A9 road 1¹/₂ miles north of Brora. The site is
on the right, signposted.

Stroma View Caravan and Camping Park `38`
Huna, John O' Groats, Wick, Caithness, Highlands,
KW1 4YL
01955 611313
Follow the A99 road to John O'Groats and turn left at
the Sea View Hotel. Follow the A836 Thurso road for
1¹/₂ miles. The site is on the left opposite the island
of Stroma.

Thurso Caravan and Camping Park `41`
Scrabster Road, Thurso, Sutherland, Highlands,
KW14 7JY
Tel: 01847 895782 / 894631
In Thurso adjacent to the A9.

Halladale Inn Caravan Park `42`
Melvich, Sutherland, KW14 7YJ
Tel: 01641 531282
www.halladaleinn.co.uk
From Thurso on the A836 to Tongue. When you get to
Melvich the site is well signposted.

Craigdhu Camping and Caravan Site `43`
Bettyhill, Sutherland, KW14 7SP
Tel: 01641 521273
On the A836 Tongue/Thurso road in the village of
Bettyhill.

Bayview Caravan Site `44`
Talmine by Lairg, Sutherland, Highlands, IV27 4YS
Tel: 01847 601225
From the A836 through Tongue across Causeway. Turn
right onto the Melness Road to Talmine and follow the
signpost to the site.

Sands Holiday Centre `54`
Gairloch, Wester Ross, Ross-shire, Highlands, IV21 2DL
Tel: 01445 712152
www.sandsholidaycentre.co.uk
Follow the A832 to Gairloch. At Gairloch take the
B8021 to Melvaig. A four mile drive will bring you to
the holiday centre.

Resipole Caravan Park `62`
Loch Sunart, Acharacle, Argyll, PH36 4HX
Tel: 01967 431235
www.resipole.co.uk
From Strontian, travel west seven miles on the A861
and the site is on the right almost on the lock shore
opposite a slipway.

Fiunary Camping and Caravan Park CS `68`
Morven, Argyll, PA34 5XX
Tel: 01967 421225
After crossing on the Corran/Ardgour car ferry. Take the
A884 toLochaline, turn right on to the B849 for 4¹/₂
miles and the site is on the left.

Peninver Sands Caravan Park `72`
Peninver, Cambeltown, Argyll, PA28 6QP
Tel: 01586 552262
www.peninver-sands.com/
From Campbeltown take the B842 road. Just before
Peninver the site is on the right.

Argyll Caravan Park `74`
Inverary, Argyll, PA32 8XT
Tel: 01499 302285
www.argyllcaravanpark.com
The site is on the A83 two miles south of Inverary.

Craig Tara Holiday Park `75`
Donure Road, Ayr, KA7 4LB
Tel: 08712 310866
www.haven.com
If you are coming from the north take the A77 towards
Stranraer. Second right after Bankfield roundabout
south of Ayr. From Doonholm road take a left at the
junction and immediate right into Greenfield Avenue.
At the next junction go left and follow signs for Heads
of Ayr.

Balkenna `77`
Girvan Road, Turnberry, Ayrshire KA26 9LN
Tel: 01655 331692
www.balkenna.co.uk
Four miles north of Girvan. Half a mile south of
Turnberry.

Castle Bay Caravan Park — 79

Portpatrick, Stranraer, DG9 9AA
Tel: 01776 810462
www.castlebayholidaypark.co.uk
From the south take the A75 from Dumfries. Entering Portpatrick take the first left hand turn past the war memorial. Continue for three quarters of of a mile, going under an old railway bridge, and in 50 yards you will reach the site entrance.

Maryport Caravan Site — 82

Mull of Galloway, Drummore, Stranraer, DG9 9RD
Tel: 01776 840 359
South on the A716 to Drummore. Follow the sign to Maryport. The site is right at the end of the road.

New England Bay Caravan Club Site — 83

Port Logan, Drummore, DG9 9NX
Tel: 01776 860275
www.caravanclub.co.uk
From the east on the A75 about two miles past Glenluce, fork left onto the B7084, signposted 'Drummore'. In about six miles continue onto the A716, signposted 'Drummore'. The site is on the left in six miles, about one mile past the B7065 junction.

Sands of Luce Holiday Park — 84

Sandhead, Stranraer, Dumfries and Galloway, DG9 9JN
Tel: 01766 830456
www.sandsofluceholidaypark.co.uk
From the A75 three miles west of Glenluce turn south onto the A716 towards Drummore. The Holiday Park is on the left approaching Sandhead.

West Barr Farm Caravan Park — 85

Port William, Newton Stewart, DG8 9QS
Tel: 01988 700367
www.westbarrholidaypark.co.uk
Two miles northwest of Port William on the A747.

Knock School Caravan Park — 86

Monreith, Newton Stewart, Wigtownshire, DG8 8NJ
Tel: 01988 700414
www.knockschool.co.uk
Located on the A747, three miles south of Port William and seven miles north of the historic town of Whithorn.

Burrowhead Holiday Village — 87

Isle of Whithorn, Newton Stewart, Dumfries and Galloway, DG8 8JB
Tel: 01988 500252
www.burrowheadholidayvillage.co.uk/
Two miles southwest of the Isle of Whithorn and 24 miles southwest of Newton Stewart.

Seaward Caravan Park — 90

Dhoon Bay, Kirkcudbright, Dumfries and Galloway, DG6 4TJ
Tel: 01557 331079
www.gillespie-leisure.co.uk
Take the A755 from Kirkcudbright for half a mile and then turn south onto the B727 towards Borgue. The site is on the right in two miles.

Queensberry Bay Holiday Park — 93

Powfoot, Annan, Dumfriesshire, DG12 5PN,
Tel: 01461 700205
www.queensberrybay.co.uk
Exit the A74(M) at Junction 22 onto the A75 and travel nine miles southwest, passing Annan. Then turn left onto the B721, signposted 'Annan' and the campsite. In 0.7 miles, turn right signposted 'Powfoot' and campsite onto the B724. Then in 2.3 miles turn left, signposted 'Powfoot 'and campsite. Follow this road to the sea and the site.

Port Bàn Holiday Park Ltd — 94

Kilberry, Argyll, PA29 6YD
Tel: 01880 770 224
www.portban.com
Travelling west on the M8, exit and go over Erskine Bridge and continue west onto the A82, signposted 'Campbeltown'. At Tarbet Loch Lomond, the road becomes the A83 as you pass the Tarbet Hotel on your right. Continue on, through Arrochar, Inveraray onto Lochgilphead, then turn left, signposted 'Campbeltown'. Pass through Ardrishaig and turn right, signposted 'Kilberry' onto the single-track B8024 road. Travel 15 miles and Port Bàn is signposted on your right.

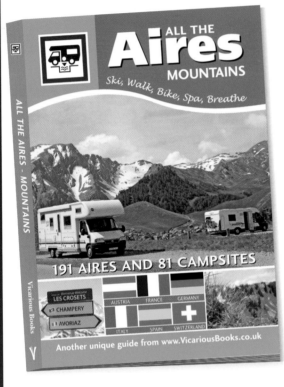

Sea Buckthorn

Campfire Cooking

Caerfai Bay, Pembrokeshire

PorthMadDog

WALES

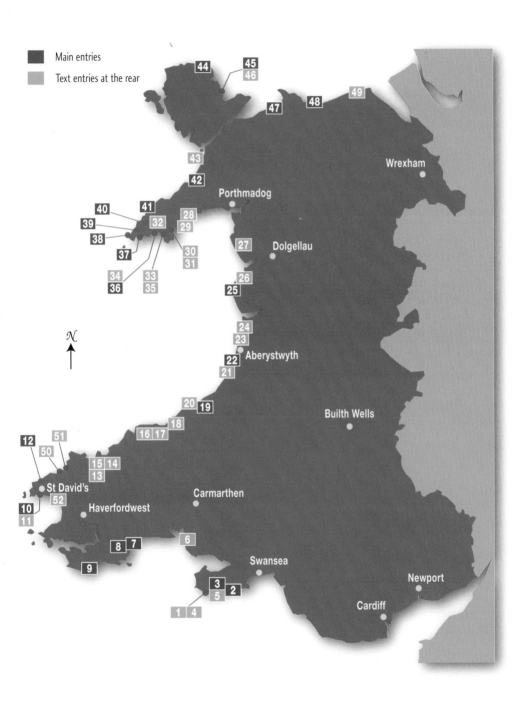

Main entries

Text entries at the rear

44
45
46
47
48
49

43
42

Wrexham

Porthmadog

40   41
39
38   32   28
        29
37   30
        31
34   33
36   35

27   Dolgellau

26
25

24
23
22   Aberystwyth
21

20   19
18
16 17

Builth Wells

12   51
50
15 14
13

St David's

10   52
11   Haverfordwest

Carmarthen

8 7
6

9

Swansea

3
5   2
1   4

Newport

Cardiff

WALES

WALES

Three Cliffs Bay Caravan Park 2

North Hills Farm, Penmaen, Gower, Swansea,
SA3 2HB Tel: 01792 371218
www.threecliffsbay.com

Excellent facilities and an absolutely superb view from most pitches over Three Cliffs Bay. The site is mostly sloping but some level ground is available. Booking is essential in school holidays. Nearby is Oxwich Bay, a sandy beach that is always popular with young families.

NA 5	NP 65	💀 8 AMP		
WC	♿	📶	🛁	📷 MG MB
🍴	🛒	📷	⚓	🚶

Pub 1 mile. Slipway 2 miles at Oxwich Bay.

££ 🐕 ♂♀ M ⓘ WiFi

The site is situated off the A4118 South Gower Road from Swansea to Port Eynon. After passing the village of Parkmill turn sharp left just on entering Penmaen. The site is signposted.

Cymru Wales ★★★★

GPS: N51°34.674'W004°06.969'
OS grid: 159 SS 543 879

April - October

Nicholaston Farm Caravan 3 and Camping Site

Nicholaston Farm, Penmaen, Gower,
SA3 2HL Tel: 01792 371209
www.nicholastonfarm.co.uk

This working farm has three fields providing mostly sloping accommodation. The showers and toilets are nicely incorporated into the farm buildings. Most pitches on the caravan field have a fine south facing view overlooking the beautiful Oxwich Bay. Access to the beach is only a short walk from the site and you can walk a couple of miles along the beach to Oxwich. Nicholaston Farm is a family campsite and does not have a bar/clubhouse but does have a farm shop, café, and Pick Your Own fruit on site.

NA 14	NP 120	💀 10 AMP		
WC	♿	📶	🛁	📷 MG MB
🍴	🛒	📷	⚓	🚶

Pub 2 miles at Oxwich.

££ 🐕 ♂♀ M ⓘ WiFi

Directions: The site is situated off the A4118 South Gower Road from Swansea to Port Eynon. Go through the village of Penmaen, then, just as you enter Nicholaston, the farm is signed on the left. Turn left down the lane and the farm is a few yards on the left. Park in the farmyard, the campsite reception is in the farm shop/café.

Cymru Wales ★★★★

GPS: N51°34.477'W004°07.991'
OS grid: 159 SS 523 884

April - October

Trevayne Farm Caravan and Camping Park [7]

Monkstone, Saundersfoot, Pembrokeshire,
SA69 9DL Tel: 01834 813402
www.camping-pembrokeshire.co.uk

This is a popular family site on a working farm. The pitches are spread over several fields so a pitch with a sea view should be requested when booking. The site facilities are very good. There is private access to the beach at Monkstone Bay, a 10 minute walk down a cliff path with steps all the way. Bass and mackerel fishing are especially good at high tide here. At low tide a large sandy beach is created, a lovely alternative to the busier beaches at Saundersfoot and Tenby, which have all the attractions you would expect of popular seaside resorts.

| NA 21 | NP 140 | 10-16 AMP |

Pub 1 mile at New Hedges. Slipway 1 1/2 miles at Saundersfoot. Note: Black water disposal down a manhole.

£££

Directions: Take the A478 south from its junction with the A477, signposted Tenby. At the New Hedges by-pass roundabout turn left onto the B4316, then take the first right into New Hedges, and turn immediately left where you see the campsite sign. The site is three quarters of a mile at the end of the road. Access/pitches for RVs: Possible.

GPS: N51°41.788'W004°41.511'
OS grid: 158 SN 141 032

Easter - October

Windmills Caravan Park [8]

Slippery Back, Tenby, Pembrokeshire,
SA70 8TJ
Tel: 01834 842200

A quiet, select site, with beautifully kept, closely mown grass. The facilities, although not new, are well kept and clean. There are good sea views over to Tenby and Caldy Island. A footpath at the site entrance takes you three quarters of a mile downhill to North Beach and Tenby. Saundersfoot and Tenby have all the attractions you would expect of popular seaside resorts and offer cafés and restaurants appealing to all tastes and budgets. The 186 mile Pembrokeshire Coast Path also runs nearby.

| NA 4 | NP 15 | 10 AMP |

Pub 1/2 mile at New Hedges. Slipway 2 miles at Saundersfoot.

£££

Directions: Travelling south on the A478 to Tenby, drive through New Hedges and turn second left into Slippery Back. The campsite is on the left.

GPS: N51°41.068'W004°42.493'
OS grid: 158 SN 128 019

April - October

WALES

Trefalen Farm

Bosherton, Pembroke, Pembrokeshire,
SA71 5DR
Tel: 01646 661643

This beautiful, informal site consists of two fields. One is mainly flat and used for caravans and motorhomes, the other is partly sloping and used mainly for tents. The site facilities, although basic, are well kept and clean. The site is peaceful and remote, but only a short distance from the unspoilt sandy beach of Broadhaven. The site is adjacent to the 186 mile Pembrokeshire Coast Path and the National Trust's Stackpole Estate.

| NA | 20 | NP | 90 | 0 AMP | | |

| WC | | | | | MG | MB |

Pub 1 mile. Shop 5 miles. Slipway 3 miles.

£££

Directions: Take the B4319 south from Pembroke and follow signs to Bosherton. In Bosherton pass the church on the left then turn left just past St Govans Country Inn, signed Broad Haven. The site is one mile down the lane just before the car park at the end of the road. Call at the white farmhouse, on the sharp left hand bend, to book in before entering the site.

GPS: N51°36.443'W004°55.635'
OS grid: 158 SR 974 939

All Year

Caerfai Bay Caravan and Tent Park

10

St David's, Haverfordwest, Pembrokeshire,
SA62 6QT Tel: 01437 720274
www.caerfaibay.co.uk

This site is popular with families and virtually every pitch has an almost 180° sea view across St Brides Bay. Facilities are excellent and spotlessly clean. The site is right on the Pembrokeshire Coast Path and it is a short walk down to beautiful Caerfai Bay beach. The St David's Peninsula is an excellent location for anyone who appreciates the beauty of unspoilt coastal scenery and countryside. The amenities of St David's are just a 10 minute walk away.

| NA | 9 | NP | 120 | 10 AMP | | |

| WC | | | | | MG | MB |

Slipway at Porthclais. Tent campers not allowed dogs July to September.

£££

Directions: From the A487 Haverfordwest to St David's road turn left just as you enter St David's, signposted Caerfai. Continue down this road and turn right before the car park.

AA
▶▶▶▶
Cymru Wales
★★★★

GPS: N51°52.382'W005°15.446'
OS grid: 157 SM 759 244

March - November

Rhosson Ganol Farm 12

St David's, Pembrokeshire,
SA62 6PY
Tel: 01437 720361

The site is spread over two fields in an idyllic, isolated location with far reaching views across to Ramsey Island. This is a popular, informal site, with some families returning year after year. The facilities are adjacent to the farmhouse across the road. Whilst not new, they are more than adequate and were newly painted and perfectly clean when we visited.

| NA 3¹/₂ | NP 41 | 0 AMP | 🚐 | |
| WC | | 🚿 | | |

Pub and shop 1¹/₂ miles at St David's.
Slipway 2 miles at Porthclais.

£££ 🐕 ♦♦ M ⓘ WiFi

Directions: From St David's head west 1¹/₂ miles, following signs to St Justinians. Pass the owner's farmhouse on the right and the campsite entrance is 100m on the left.

GPS: N51°52.721'W005°18.287'
OS grid: 157 SM 726 252

Easter - October

Cei Bach Country Club Touring and Tenting Park 19

Parc-Y-Brwcs, Cei Bach, New Quay,
Ceredigion, SA45 9SL Tel: 01545 580237
www.cei-bach.co.uk

This well kept site overlooks Cei Bach Bay, a very attractive, sheltered, sandy bathing beach. Many of the pitches have a sea view and there are numerous attractions nearby. From the site a pathway leads to the beach and a coastal path to Aberaeron, which passes over a waterfall on the way.

| NA 3 | NP 60 | 10 AMP | 🚐 | 🚐 |
| WC | | 🚿 | 🔥 | MG | MB |

Slipway 2 miles at New Quay.

£££ 🐕 ♦♦ M ⓘ WiFi

Directions: From the A487 coast road turn northwest at Llanarth, on the B4342 by the Llanina Arms pub. Travel two miles, passing the Schooner Park caravan site, and turn right at the crossroads. Follow the narrow lane, just short of one mile, to the site.
RVs: Possible.

GPS: N52°12.660'W004°19.886'
OS grid: 146 SN 408 595

1st March - 8th January

WALES

Morfa Bychan Holiday Park 22

Llanfarian, Aberystwyth, Ceredigion,
SY23 4QQ Tel: 01970 617254
www.hillandale.co.uk

This well maintained holiday site has good facilities.
Most touring pitches are sloping, but all have a wide
view of the sea. The attractive reception/shop has
friendly, helpful staff and stocks basic essentials. There
is direct access from site to a private pebble beach.

NA	3	NP	65	10 AMP		
WC					MG	MB

Pub 2 miles at Llanfarian. Slipway 5 miles at Aberystwyth.

£££

Directions: The easiest access to the site is from the
south. Take the A487 coast road north from
Aberaeron. About four miles north of Llanrhystud turn
off to the left and follow the tourist signs for about
two miles to the site. Access/pitches for RVs: Possible.

GPS: N52°22.354'W004°06.020'
OS grid: 135 SN 157 766

All Year

Cae-Du Campsite 25

Cae-Du, Rhoslefain, Tywyn,
Gwynedd, LL36 9ND
Tel: 01654 711234

This is an idyllic location, perfect to get away from it
all. The site has good facilities and is divided into
several areas. Some pitches are almost on the beach
and some are at higher levels but all have a fine view
across the sea. The site has a very relaxed atmosphere
and open fires are allowed. It's a real pleasure to find
that on such an informal site, the facilities are quite
modern and beautifully kept.

NA	10	NP	65	0 AMP		
WC					MG	MB

Shop 4 miles at Bryncrug. Slipway 7 miles at Tywyn.

£££

Directions: Take the A493 coast road south from
Fairbourne. Drive through Llwyngwril, continue for 2³/₄
miles turning right off the main road at the sharp left-
hand bend. Go down the steep track and stop at the
farm to book in. If coming from the Aberdyfi direction
with a motorhome or caravan it is better to go past the
site and turn round in the next lay-by. Slightly tight
access down a rough track passing under a railway bridge.

GPS: N52°37.992'W004°06.971'
OS grid: 124 SH 569 059

March - October

36
Treheli Farm Campsite

Treheli, Rhiw, Pwllheli, Gwynedd, LL53 8AA
Tel: 01758 780281

This is one of those sites people keep returning to, the relaxed atmosphere and fabulous view right across Porth Neigwl (Hells Mouth Bay) makes it a must. The site is on a narrow strip above the bay and the view is uninterrupted. Open fires are allowed on certain parts of the site. The basic facilities are adjacent to the farmhouse where there is also a spring water tap. A steep walk leads down to the beach, a long stretch of sand and stones, exposed to the full force of the Atlantic. Though popular with surfers the beach seldom gets busy. Note that bathing can be dangerous here, with strong undertows and cross currents.

| NA | 1 1/2 | NP | 27 | 0 AMP | |
| WC | | | | | MG | MB |

Pub 4 miles at Abersoch. Slipway 4 miles at Aberdaron.

£££ 🐕 ♀♂ M ⓘ WiFi

Directions: Take the A449 from Pwllheli to Llanbedrog, at Llanbedrog turn right onto the B4413. Continue on the B4413 through Mynytho, just after the village bear left then after approx three miles turn right. The site is a few hundred yards on the left, opposite the farm. Call at the farmhouse before pitching.

GPS: N52°49.541'W004°36.671'
OS grid: 123 SH 242 285

March - October

37
Morfa Mawr Farm

Morfa Mawr Farm, Aberdaron, Pwllheli, Gwynedd, LL53 8BD
Tel: 01758 760264

This farm site spreads over two fields, the larger is flat and set aside for tents only, but both have fabulous views over Aberdaron Bay. Onsite facilities are maintained to a good standard and there is access directly to the beach, which is about a three minute walk downhill.

| NA | 3 | NP | 53 | 6 AMP | |
| WC | | | | | MG | MB |

Pub, shop and slipway 2/3 mile at Aberdaron.

£££ 🐕 ♀♂ M ⓘ WiFi

Directions: From Aberdaron, take the coastal road signposted Rhiw. The site is down the first track on the right, about two thirds of a mile from Aberdaron.

GPS: N52°48.333'W004°41.842'
OS grid: 123 SH 184 263

March - October

Mynydd Mawr 38
Camping and Caravan Site

Llanllawen Fawr, Aberdaron, Pwllheli, Gwynedd,
LL53 8BY Tel: 01758 760223
www.aberdaroncaravanandcampingsite.co.uk

Gloriously isolated, this informal site has the most wonderful views, including a great view to the sea in two directions. Right on the edge of the National Trust protected area, the accommodation is comprised of one flat and one partly sloping field. The facilities, although basic, are clean and well kept, with the unexpected bonus of two 'family bathrooms' complete with shower, toilet and basin. There are good walks in the area and the adjoining headland is a popular attraction for walkers.

| NA | 1 1/4 | NP | 30 | 6 AMP |

| WC |

Shop 2 miles at Aberdaron.

£££   WiFi

Directions: Fork right off the B4413 (Llanbedrog - Aberdaron) about 3 1/4 miles past Pen-Y-Groeslan. In about one mile take the right turn, signposted Uwchmynydd. Carry on, past the chapel on the right, and the site is about one mile further on the left. (Approximately a quarter of a mile past the Ty-Newydd campsite). A map with directions can be found on the site's website.

GPS: N52°47.703'W004°45.353'
OS grid: 123 SH 143 255

March - October

Ty-Newydd Farm 39
Caravan and Camping Site

Uwchmynydd, Aberdaron, Gwynedd,
LL53 8BY Tel: 01758 760581
www.tynewyddfarm-site.co.uk

This is a tidy and well cared for site popular with families. The small on-site café cooks all day breakfasts and afternoon cream teas. There is a fine view across to Bardsey Island and plenty of good walking in the area. Much of the coast is owned by the National Trust. The adjoining headland is a popular attraction ideal for walks. The surrounding views are delightful with stunning sunsets, panoramic views of mountains and seascapes, creating a peaceful and relaxing atmosphere.

| NA | 5 | NP | 30 | 6 AMP |

| WC |

Pub, shop and slipway 2 miles at Aberdaron.

£££   WiFi

Directions: Fork right off the B4413 (Llanbedrog - Aberdaron) about 3 1/4 miles past Pen-Y-Groeslan. In about one mile take the right turn, signposted Uwchmynydd. Carry on, past the chapel on the right, and the site is about three quarters of a mile further on the left.

Cymru
Wales

★★★

GPS: N52°47.835'W004°45.078'
OS grid: 123 SH 146 257

March - October

Plasffordd CL **40**

Plasffordd, Aberdaron, Pwllheli, LL53 8LL
Tel: 01758 760439
www.caravanclub.co.uk

A flat site with a distant view of the sea. This site is quiet, secluded and very reasonably priced. Across from the site entrance are a house, where a toilet and shower are available. Access to the sea is about one mile away, at Whistling Sands.

NA	3/4	NP	5		16 AMP		
WC							

Pub, shop and slipway 1 1/2 miles at Aberdaron.

£££

Directions: Fork right off the B4413 at Llanbedrog - Aberdaron. Travel on the B4417 towards Aberdaron, passing the Aberdaron boundary sign, and fork right by the council houses (200 yards past river/bridge). Turn right at the cross roads, signposted for 'Whistling Sands'. Site is one mile further on.

GPS: N52°49.299'W004°43.728'
OS grid: 123 SH 162 284

April - October

Llecyn Llangwnadl **41**

Llecyn Llangwnadl, Pwllheli,
Gwynedd, LL53 8NT
Tel: 01758 770347

Located on a working farm, this is a tidy and basic family site with a view of the sea over the hedges. Access to the beautiful and isolated Penllech Beach is about half a mile down the footpath opposite the site entrance.

NA	4	NP	35		6 AMP		
WC							

Shop 1/4 mile and 3 miles. Slipway 1/4 mile.

£££

Directions: From Pwllheli take the A495 to Morfa Nefyn, then take the B4412 through Edern and Tudweilog to Llangwnadl. Turn right towards Porth Colman, follow the Porth Colman signs and the site is on the left in about 1 1/4 miles down a narrow lane. RVs: Possible.

GPS: N52°52.271'W004°40.816'
OS grid: 123 SH 194 342

Easter - October

Aberafon [42]
Camping and Caravan Site

Gyrn Goch, Caernarfon, Gwynedd,
LL54 5PN Tel: 01286 660295
www.aberafon.co.uk

Beautifully located, this site has pitches in a sheltered valley, some on a large field adjacent to and overlooking the sea and some almost on its own private bathing beach. The surroundings are altogether delightful, with panoramic views and seascapes, creating a peaceful relaxing atmosphere, but also ideal for children to play and explore. The site is at the foot of the 1,500 ft Gyrn Goch mountain. There is good river fishing nearby along with excellent mountain and coastal walks.

| NA | 10 | | NP | 65 | | 10 AMP | | |

| WC | | | | | | | | |

Shop and pub 1 mile at Clynnog-fawr. Slipway on site.

£££

Directions: From Caernarfon, take the A487 south to Llanwnda. At the roundabout, bear right onto the A499. Go through the village of Clynnog-Fawr, then in about one mile, at Gyrn Goch, turn right at a red shed into a narrow lane. The campsite is at the end of the lane. Warning: the lane is very narrow and not suitable for large vans.

GPS: N53°00.548'W004°23.166'
OS grid: 123 SH 400 484

March - October

Tyddyn Isaf [44]
Caravan and Camping Park

Lligwy Bay, Dulas, Isle of Angelsey,
LL70 9PQ Tel: 01248 410203
www.tyddynisaf.co.uk

A family run, spacious and well laid out hillside site with excellent security. The touring pitches are on the upper part of the site and most benefit from a fine sea view. There is a large children's play area and the owners have planted thousands of trees and shrubs to create a conservation area and haven for wildlife. The beach at Lligwy Bay is just 250 yards away along the site's own private footpath. Cycle and kayak hire available on the beach in summer.

| NA | 22 | | NP | 42 | | 10 AMP | | |

| WC | | | | | | | | |

Slipway 2 miles.

£££

Directions: Cross the Britannia Bridge onto Anglesey, and take the second exit, A5025, marked Benllech/Amlwch. At the top of the slip road turn right. Follow the A5025 through Pentraeth and Benellech then at second roundabout turn left. After one mile, at Brynefail, turn right opposite the telephone box. Follow the signs for Tyddyn Isaf down the narrow lane. The site entrance is half a mile on the right.

GPS: N53°21.758'W004°16.535'
OS grid: 114 SH 487 875

April - September

Dafarn Rhos Caravan and Camping Site `45`

Lligwy Beach, Moelfre, Isle of Anglesey, LL72 8NN Tel: 01248 410607
www.dafarnrhos.wanadoo.co.uk

A friendly family site with beautiful views over Lligwy Bay. The site is partly sloping, but many pitches are level and the majority have a sea view. The main toilet and shower facilities are in portacabins that were new in 2007 and are immaculately kept. During the summer, kayak and cycle hire is available on the beach two minutes from site. Sometimes seals and their pups, and even dolphins, can be seen close to shore. The coast path follows the cliffs both ways, and there is also a designated cycle path that goes past the campsite.

| NA 3.1 | NP 85 | 16 AMP |

| WC | | | | | MG | MB |

Pub and shop 1 mile at Moelfre. Slipway 200m.

£££ WiFi

Directions: Cross the Britannia Bridge onto Anglesey, and take the second exit, A5025, marked Benllech/Amlwch. Continue through Benllech on the A5025 and, at the roundabout, take the second exit to Moelfre. Continue downhill and take the first left after the fish and chip shop. Travel for one mile to a crossroads and turn right into the dead end road, and the site is on the left through a gate. Do not rely solely on GPS!

GPS: N53°21.419'W004°15.657'
OS grid: 114 SH 499 864

March - October

Tyddyn Du Touring Park `47`

Conwy Old Road, Penmaenmawr, LL34 6RE
Tel: 01492 622300
www.tyddyndutouringpark.co.uk

A beautifully kept, adults only (over 18) site with panoramic views across Conwy Bay to The Great Orme at Llandudno and over to Anglesey and Puffin Island. Snowdonia National Park is easily accessed with glorious walks for the beginner and enthusiast. An award winning beach is about 15 minutes walk away. The campsite has excellent facilities including a well equipped utility/laundry room. The Championship golf course at Conwy is a couple of miles away and Penmaenmawr's delightful golf course is just 200m away.

| NA 5 | NP 100 | 16 AMP |

| WC | | | | | MG | MB |

Pub 100 yards. Shop 1/2 mile. Beach 10 minutes. Slipway 1 mile.

£££ WiFi

Directions: Take the A55 west from Conwy for five miles, then turn left at the Penmaenmawr roundabout, Junction 16. Turn immediately left and the site entrance is about 300 yards on the right, after The Gladstone pub. Maximum caravan/motorhome size 7.5m (25ft).

Cymru Wales
★★★★

GPS: N53°16.593'W003°54.369'
OS grid: 115 SH 730 772

March - October

WALES

Bron-Y-Wendon Touring Park

Wern Road, Llanddulas, Colwyn Bay,
LL22 8HG Tel: 01492 512903
www.northwales-holidays.co.uk

This is a very well kept site, with the pitches organised in small groups. All the pitches enjoy a beautiful coastal view and the beach is only a short walk away. Llanddulas village has shops and pubs and nearby the long Promenade follows the vast sweep from Old Colwyn to Penrhyn Bay, giving easy access to the wonderful beaches, pier and harbour at Rhos-on-Sea, which are all joined by a cycle track. Slipways are situated along the promenade for fishing, sailing, and jet skiing.

NA 8   NP 130   16 AMP

WC

Pub, shop and beach 1/2 a mile.

£££   M   WiFi

Directions: Take the A55 into north Wales and turn off at Junction 25 for Llanddulas. Then take the first right, back under the A55 and follow the brown tourist signs for the caravan park, located on the left.

AA ►►►► ★★★★★

Cymru Wales

GPS: N53°17.508'W003°38.763'
OS grid: 116 SH 904 785

All Year

Carreglwyd Camping and Caravan Park 1
The Seafront, Port Eynon, SA3 1NN
Tel: 01792 390795
www.carreglwyd.com
Follow the A4118 from Swansea to Port Eynon a distance of about 18 miles. Carreglwyd is situated adjacent to the village and sandy beach.

Bank Farm 4
Horton, Gower Peninsula, SA3 1LL
Tel: 01792 390228
www.bankfarmleisure.co.uk
Follow the A4118 pass through Knelston and Scurlage. One mile after Scurlage, turn left for Horton at Moor Corner Farm. The entrance is 100 yards on the right.

Greenways Holiday Park 5
Oxwich, SA3 1LY
Tel: 01792 390220
www.greenwayleisure.co.uk
Take the A4118 from Swansea to Port Eynon road. One mile past Nicholaston turn left signposted 'Nature Reserve' and follow the two mile, narrow and steep drive to the campsite.

Carmarthen Bay Touring and Camping Park 6
Tanylan Farm, Kidwelly, Carmarthenshire, SA17 5HJ
Tel: 01267 267306
www.tanylanfarmholidays.co.uk
From Junction 48 of the M4 follow signs to Pembury Country Park. At Pembury on the A484, follow signs to Kidwelly. Turn at the Spar shop and, after 400 yards, turn left onto the coastal road. Continue for two miles and the camping park is on the right.

Rhos-Y-Cribed 11
St Davids, Pembrokeshire, SA62 6RR
Tel: 01437 720336
One mile southwest of St. David's on the road to Porthclais Harbour.

Gwaun Vale Holiday Touring Park 13
Llanychaer, Fishguard, Pembrokeshire, SA65 9TA
Tel: 01348 874698
www.gwaunvale.co.uk

At the roundabout where the A40 Haverfordwest road meets the A487 road to Cardigan, take the road marked Aberguan and Fishguard. Travel through Fishguard and turn left at the roundabout, passing Barclay's and the Town Hall. Turn right at Hamilton Street, following the brown camping signs. You will see a sign on the right indicating Gwaun Vale is in a mile to the left. Turn left at Park Street as the sign indicates and travel one mile, staying to the left and following signs for Gwaun Valley.

Morawelon Camping and Caravan Site · 14

Parog, Newport, SA42 0RW
Tel: 01239 820565
In Newport. Heading east on the A487, turn left at the brown camping sign, Parrog Road. Follow to the end.

Tycanol Farm · 15

Newport, SA42 0ST
Tel: 01239 820264
www.caravancampingsites.co.uk/pembrokeshire/tycanolfarm
500 yards northwest of the A487. One mile west of Newport.

Blaenwaun Farm · 16

Mwnt, Cardigan, Ceredigion, SA43 1QF
Tel: 01239 613456
www.blaenwaunfarm.com
Travelling north from Cardigan on the B4548 towards Gwbent and Mwnt. Take the first right for Mwnt and follow the signs.

Dolgelynen Caravan Park · 17

B4333, Aberporth,Ceredigion SA43 2HL
Tel: 01239 811095
Located half a mile southeast of Aberporth on the B4333.

Llety Caravan Park · 18

Tresaith, Ceredigion, SA43 2ED
Tel: 01239 810354
www.ukparks.co.uk/llety
From Aberystwyth, on the A487 to Cardigan, turn right onto the B4333 to Aberporth. Take the next turning right signposted, Tresaith. The Llety Caravan Park is on the left in about a mile.

Aeron Coast Caravan Park · 20

North Road, Aberaeron, Ceredigion, SA46 0JF
Tel: 01545 570349
www.aeroncoast.co.uk
On the northern edge of the Aberaeron main coastal road take the A487. The site is 200 yards from the town centre and harbour.

Pengarreg Caravan Park · 21

Llanrhystud, Aberystwyth, Ceredigion, SY23 5DH
Tel: 01974 202247
www.utowcaravans.co.uk/pengarreg.htm
Nine miles south of Aberystwyth and just off the A487 in the village of Llanrhystud, opposite a service station.

Ocean View Holiday Park · 23

Clarach Bay, Aberystwyth, SY23 3DL
Tel: 01970 828425/01970 623361
www.oceanviewholidays.com
From Aberystwyth travel three miles to Bow Street on the A487. Turn left to Clarach Bay and Llangorwen on the B4572 then follow signs to the beach.

Pen-Y-Graig Farm Caravan Park · 24

Borth, Dyfed, SY24 5NR
Tel: 01970 871717
Take the A487 three miles north of Abery to Bow Street. Turn left onto the B4353 at Rhydypennav, and travel through Landre for about four miles. At Borth, turn left at the lifeboat station and continue up the hill on Clarach Road. At the top of the hill turn right. Travel down the lane for about 200 yards and turn right at the T-junction, follow the country lane to the site.

Hendre Hall · 26

Llwyngwril, Gwynedd, LL37 2JF
Tel: 01341 250322
On the A493 Dolgellau-Tywyn Road, opposite the petrol station in Llwyngwril.

WALES

Trawsdir Touring Caravan and Camping Site 27
Llanaber, Barmouth, Gwynedd, LL42 1RR
Tel: 01341 280999
www.trawsdir.co.uk
In Cardigan Bay, two miles north of Barmouth on the
A496 Harlech Road. Seven miles from Harlech Castle.

Sarn Farm 28
Sarn Bach, Pwllheli, Gwynedd, LL53 5BG
Tel: 01758 713583
http://sarn-farm-caravan-and-camping-site.wales.info
Take the A499 from Pwllheli to Abersoch and continue
south to Sarn Bach. The site is the first farm on the left
in Sarn Bach.

Beach View Caravan and Camping Park 29
Bwlchtocyn, Abersoch, LL53 7BT
Tel: 01758 712956
From Abersoch, take the A499 road to Sarn Bach over
the crossroads at the top of the hill. Turn left past the
post office and church, then take the left turning
signposted, 'Beach View'. The site is on the left in three
quarters of a mile.

Caerau Farm 30
Aberdaron, Pwllheli, LL53 8BG
Tel: 01758 760481
On the B4413 at Pwllheli, take the A499 to Abersoch.
At Llanbedrog, turn right and take the B4413,
signposted 'Aberdaron'. Follow the main road through
the villages and, after Rhoshirwaun, Caeraw Farm is on
the left-hand side on the outskirts of Aberdaron.

Bryn Bach Campsite 31
Tyddyn Talgoch Uchaf, Bwlchtocyn, Nr Abersoch,
Gwynedd, LL53 7BT
Tel: 01758 712285
www.abersochcamping.co.uk/acc.html
From the A499 in Abersoch, follow Lon Sarn Bach for
one mile, towards Bwlchtocyn. Turn left at the brown
sign indicating Gwesty Porth Tocyn Hotel. Travel three
quarters of a mile, following signs, and the site is on
your left. The road is narrow in places with some
passing areas.

Cefn Hedog 32
Rhoshirwaun, Pwllheli, Gwynedd, LL53 8HL
Tel: 01758 760551   07799 282846
www.cefnhedog.co.uk
Take the B4413 Llanbedrog to Aberdaron road for
about seven miles. Go straight across the crossroads at
Pen y Groeslon and take the first right signposted to
Whistling Sands. The site is the first driveway on the
right.

Cilan Riding Centre 33
Cilan Fawr, Cilan, Abersoch, LL53 7DD
Tel: 01758 713276
www.abersochholidays.net
Take the A499 from Pwllheli to Abersoch. From the
centre of Abersoch, take the road out of the village to
Sarn Bach. Continue for one mile, past a chapel and
telephone kiosk on your right. Take the first right
turning and continue down the lane to Cilan Fawr, which
is on the left at the end of the lane. Ask for Emlyn
and Hilda.

Seaview/Trem-Y-Mor Caravan and Camping Park 34
Sarn Bach, LL53 7ET
Tel: 07967 050170
www.tggroup.co.uk/index.php/holidays-a-leisure
Take the A499 from Pwllheli to Abersoch, following
signs to Sarn Bach through Abersoch. After
approximately one mile, take the left turn at the
crossroads. The site is 250 yards along the lane on the
right-hand side.

Deucoch Touring and Camping Site 35
Sarn Bach, Abersoch, LL53 7LD
Tel: 01758 713293
www.deucoch.com
Travel one mile south from Abersoch to Sarn Bach and
turn right at the crossroads. The site is 500m on the
right.

St Ives Touring Caravan Site 43
Lon-Y-Wig, Pontllyfni, LL54 5EG
Tel: 01286 660347
Take the A487 from Caernarfon for approximately three

miles. Then take the A499 to Pwllheli for five miles to Pontllyfni and take the first right turn.

Bodafon Caravan Park 46
Bellech, Angelsea, LL74 8RU
Tel: 01248 852417
www.bodafonpark.co.uk
On the Isle of Anglesey, half a mile north of Bellech on the A5025.

Nant Mill Touring Caravan and Tent Park 49
Nant Mill Farm, Gronant Road, Prestatyn, Denbighshire, LL19 9LY
Tel: 01745 852360
On the A548 half a mile east of Prestatyn near the junction of the A548 and A4574. The site is four miles east of Rhyl.

Celtic Camping 50
Pwll Caerog Farm, Berea, Nr St David's, Haverfordwest, Pembrokeshire, SA62 6DG
Tel: 01348 837 405
http://celtic-camping.co.uk

From Croesgoch on the A487 travel 1 1/2 miles northwest on Aberelddy Road towards Morawel and Aberelddy. Pass St David's Camping and Caravanning Club site and turn left at the T-junction. In one mile turn right into a dead end road (clearly signed) and follow to the campsite.

St Davids Camping and Caravanning Club Site 51
Dwr Cwmwdig Berea, St Davids, Haverfordwest, Pembrokeshire, SA62 6DW
Tel: 01348 831376
From Croesgoch on the A487 travel 1 1/2 miles northwest on Aberelddy Road towards Morawel and Aberelddy. Pass St David's Camping and Caravanning Club site on the right and turn right at the T-junction to the site entrance.

Newgale Camping Site 52
Wood Farm, Newgale, Haverfordwest, Pembrokeshire, SA62 6AR
Tel: 01437 710253
www.newgalecampingsite.co.uk
Adjacent to the A487 at Newgale beach.

Caerfai Bay Campsite © Gill Sadler

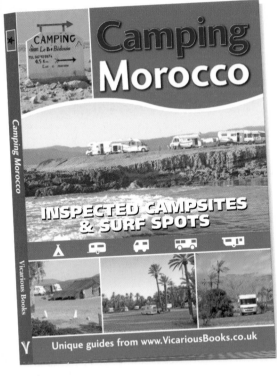

Europa Park

PUBLIC FOOTPATH
www.somerset.gov.uk

WEST SOMERSET
COAST PATH

HAPPY CAMPING

BROADSANDS BEACH
150m THEN 220 STEPS

PZ 741

INDEX

INDEX

INDEX

www.vicariousBooks.co.uk

INDEX

CAMPSITE SUBMISSION FORM

Please use this form to update the site information in this guide. We particularly need good photographs that represent the site and where possible show the sea view. Nominations for new sites are very welcome. If site is already listed, complete only sections where changes apply. Please fill in answers in capital letters and circle appropriate symbols.

Site Name:

Address:

Postcode:

Tel. No:

Website:

Units accepted by campsite *Please circle 1 or more symbols as appropriate*

Ⓐ Tent   🚐 Touring caravan   🚐 Motorhome

🚌 Large vehicles   🚐 Holiday accommodation for hire

Description of site:

NA Number of acres: NP Number of pitches:

⚡ Electricity available and amperage:

Symbols, facilities *Please circle as appropriate*

🚐 Level pitches   🚐 All season/hard standing pitches   WC Toilets   ♿ Disabled toilets

🚿 Showers   🛁 Family bathroom/ shower room   🧺 Laundry   🛁 Dishwashing facilities

MG Motorhome grey water disposal   MB Motorhome toilet waste disposal

Symbols, amenities *Please circle as appropriate*

🍺 Pub/bar   🛒 Shop   🏖 Beach   ⚓ Slipway

🎢 Children's play area   🚶 Footpath   🏊 Swimming pool indoor or outdoor

Please see overleaf

CAMPSITE SUBMISSION FORM

Please circle as appropriate

Cost based on two people, one caravan or motorhome with electric in August. Guide prices only.

£   Up to £10 per night   **££**   £10-17 per night

£££ £17-35 per night   **££££** £35 plus per night

♀ Dogs allowed onsite   **♀♀** Adults (Over 18) only   **M** Members only

CS Certified Site   **CL** Certified Location

(i) Internet available   **WiFi** WiFi Available

Directions to site:

....

....

....

Awards: Tourist Board and AA etc. *See page 12 for more information.*

....

OS grid references – 1:50,000

....

GPS Coordinates in the following format: N49°14.988' W000°16.838'

....

Opening and closing dates:

Photo(s) included: ☐ None   ☐ Emailed   ☐ Photo(s) posted with form

email pictures to: gomotorhoming@hotmail.co.uk

Name and email or address - so information can be credited:

....

Please use a separate form for each campsite. Send completed forms to:

Vicarious books, 62 Tontine Street, Folkestone, Kent, CT20 1JP

ask@vicariousbooks.co.uk

Thank you very much for your time.

By supplying details and photographs you are giving unrestricted publication and reproduction rights to Vicarious Books Ltd.

CAMPSITE SUBMISSION FORM

Please use this form to update the site information in this guide. We particularly need good photographs that represent the site and where possible show the sea view. Nominations for new sites are very welcome. If site is already listed, complete only sections where changes apply. Please fill in answers in capital letters and circle appropriate symbols.

Site Name:

Address:

Postcode:

Tel. No:

Website:

Units accepted by campsite *Please circle 1 or more symbols as appropriate*

🏕 Tent   🚐 Touring caravan   🚍 Motorhome

🚌 Large vehicles   🚐 Holiday accommodation for hire

Description of site:

NA Number of acres: **NP** Number of pitches:

⚡ Electricity available and amperage:

Symbols, facilities *Please circle as appropriate*

🅿 Level pitches   🅿 All season/hard standing pitches   **WC** Toilets   ♿ Disabled toilets

🚿 Showers   🛁 Family bathroom/ shower room   ▣ Laundry   🍽 Dishwashing facilities

MG Motorhome grey water disposal   **MB** Motorhome toilet waste disposal

Symbols, amenities *Please circle as appropriate*

🍺 Pub/bar   🏪 Shop   🏖 Beach   ⛵ Slipway

🛝 Children's play area   🚶 Footpath   🏊 Swimming pool indoor or outdoor

Please see overleaf

CAMPSITE SUBMISSION FORM

Please circle as appropriate

Cost based on two people, one caravan or motorhome with electric in August. Guide prices only.

£	Up to £10 per night	**££**	£10-17 per night
£££	£17-35 per night	**££££**	£35 plus per night

⋔ Dogs allowed onsite   **♯♯** Adults (Over 18) only   **M** Members only

CS Certified Site   **CL** Certified Location

ⓘ Internet available   WiFi WiFi Available

Directions to site:

....

....

....

....

Awards: Tourist Board and AA etc. *See page 12 for more information.*

....

OS grid references – 1:50,000

....

GPS Coordinates in the following format: N49°14.988' W000°16.838'

....

Opening and closing dates:

Photo(s) included: ☐ None   ☐ Emailed   ☐ Photo(s) posted with form

email pictures to: gomotorhoming@hotmail.co.uk

Name and email or address - so information can be credited:

....

Please use a separate form for each campsite. Send completed forms to:

Vicarious books, 62 Tontine Street, Folkestone, Kent, CT20 1JP

ask@vicariousbooks.co.uk

Thank you very much for your time.

By supplying details and photographs you are giving unrestricted publication and reproduction rights to Vicarious Books Ltd.

CAMPSITE SUBMISSION FORM

Please use this form to update the site information in this guide. We particularly need good photographs that represent the site and where possible show the sea view. Nominations for new sites are very welcome. If site is already listed, complete only sections where changes apply. Please fill in answers in capital letters and circle appropriate symbols.

Site Name:

Address:

Postcode:

Tel. No:

Website:

Units accepted by campsite *Please circle 1 or more symbols as appropriate*

Ａ Tent

Touring caravan

Motorhome

Large vehicles

Holiday accommodation for hire

Description of site:

NA Number of acres:

NP Number of pitches:

Electricity available and amperage:

Symbols, facilities *Please circle as appropriate*

Level pitches

All season/hard standing pitches

WC Toilets

Disabled toilets

Showers

Family bathroom/ shower room

Laundry

Dishwashing facilities

MG Motorhome grey water disposal

MB Motorhome toilet waste disposal

Symbols, amenities *Please circle as appropriate*

Pub/bar

Shop

Beach

Slipway

Children's play area

Footpath

Swimming pool indoor or outdoor

Please see overleaf

CAMPSITE SUBMISSION FORM

Please circle as appropriate

Cost based on two people, one caravan or motorhome with electric in August. Guide prices only.

£   Up to £10 per night   **££**   £10-17 per night

£££ £17-35 per night   **££££** £35 plus per night

🐕   Dogs allowed onsite   **††**   Adults (Over 18) only   **M**   Members only

CS   Certified Site   **CL**   Certified Location

ⓘ   Internet available   **WiFi**   WiFi Available

Directions to site:

Awards: Tourist Board and AA etc. *See page 12 for more information.*

OS grid references – 1:50,000

GPS Coordinates in the following format: N49°14.988' W000°16.838'

Opening and closing dates:

Photo(s) included: ☐ None   ☐ Emailed   ☐ Photo(s) posted with form

email pictures to: gomotorhoming@hotmail.co.uk

Name and email or address - so information can be credited:

Please use a separate form for each campsite. Send completed forms to:

Vicarious books, 62 Tontine Street, Folkestone, Kent, CT20 1JP

ask@vicariousbooks.co.uk

Thank you very much for your time.

By supplying details and photographs you are giving unrestricted publication and reproduction rights to Vicarious Books Ltd1.